Nature-Based Solutions and Circular Design: Regenerative Strategies for Climate, Biodiversity, and Resilient Systems

Copyright

Nature-Based Solutions and Circular Design: Regenerative Strategies for Climate, Biodiversity, and Resilient Systems

eBook ISBN: 978-1-991369-45-1

Paperback ISBN: 978-1-991369-46-8

Published by Global Climate Solutions.

Design and layout by Global Climate Solutions.

First edition, 2025.

Table of Contents

Introduction

Nature-based Solutions (NBS) and circular design have emerged as critical strategies in the pursuit of sustainable, resilient, and regenerative systems. In response to rising environmental pressures, these approaches emphasize working with natural processes and designing out waste to support long-term ecological and societal well-being. Together, they offer a framework for addressing the interconnected challenges of biodiversity loss, resource depletion, and climate change.

NBS are actions that protect, sustainably manage, and restore natural or modified ecosystems while delivering benefits for both human well-being and biodiversity. These solutions enhance ecosystem services, such as water purification, carbon sequestration, and temperature regulation, through the use of green infrastructure, ecological restoration, and sustainable land management. By relying on the inherent regenerative capacity of nature, NBS contribute to both climate mitigation and adaptation goals.

Circular design, as a principle of the circular economy, seeks to eliminate the concept of waste by designing systems in which resources are continuously reused, repurposed, or regenerated. Applied to built environments, products, and natural systems, circular design supports closed-loop resource flows and minimizes environmental impact. When integrated with NBS, circular design principles help maximize the efficiency and effectiveness of nature-based interventions by ensuring that material and energy flows are aligned with natural cycles.

The convergence of these two approaches enables the creation of regenerative systems that go beyond sustainability to actively restore ecosystems, enhance biodiversity, and build adaptive capacity to climate risks. This alignment also promotes multifunctional landscapes and infrastructures that deliver multiple co-benefits across environmental, economic, and social dimensions. As urban areas grow and climate-related impacts intensify, the integration of

NBS and circular design becomes increasingly relevant for shaping resilient communities and ecosystems.

This book provides a comprehensive exploration of how NBS and circular design can be deployed to drive systemic transformation. It examines the theoretical underpinnings of each concept, the practical considerations for implementation, and the governance, financial, and social dimensions that influence success. The chapters are organized to progressively build understanding, starting with foundational principles and advancing through applications in biodiversity, climate action, ecosystem services, governance, finance, and equity.

Importantly, the book does not focus on isolated examples or case studies. Instead, it offers a structured analysis of the processes, strategies, and enabling conditions that support the mainstreaming of circular nature-based approaches. The objective is to present a unified framework that links ecological design, climate resilience, and systemic regeneration.

The intended audience includes policymakers, urban planners, environmental professionals, designers, researchers, and anyone interested in advancing integrated solutions for sustainability and climate resilience. By combining the logic of circular systems with the restorative power of nature, this book contributes to a growing body of knowledge that supports innovative responses to the environmental challenges of our time.

Chapter 1: Foundations of NBS and Circular Design

This chapter introduces the core concepts that underpin the integration of NBS and circular design. It outlines the definitions, principles, and objectives of each approach, establishing a shared foundation for the chapters that follow. As climate change, biodiversity loss, and resource constraints place growing pressure on urban and rural systems alike, there is increasing recognition of the need for solutions that are both ecologically regenerative and resource-efficient.

NBS leverage natural processes and ecosystems to address societal challenges while delivering co-benefits such as enhanced biodiversity, climate resilience, and human well-being. Circular design, by contrast, focuses on minimizing waste and keeping materials, products, and resources in use for as long as possible. Although conceptually distinct, both approaches share common goals of sustainability, system thinking, and long-term value creation.

By exploring their synergies, this chapter sets the stage for understanding how NBS and circular design can be combined to support integrated, multifunctional, and scalable responses to complex environmental and social issues.

Introduction to NBS and Circular Design

NBS and circular design represent two complementary frameworks for addressing environmental challenges in a resource-efficient and regenerative manner. While originating from distinct schools of thought, both approaches share a focus on systems thinking, long-term sustainability, and integration across ecological, social, and economic domains. Together, they offer a coherent pathway toward restoring natural systems, enhancing biodiversity, and building resilience to climate-related risks.

NBS are defined as actions that protect, manage, or restore ecosystems to address societal challenges while simultaneously providing benefits to biodiversity and human well-being. They are grounded in the understanding that ecosystems, when healthy and functioning, deliver essential services such as water filtration, climate regulation, food production, and hazard mitigation. NBS are increasingly recognized as viable alternatives or complements to traditional infrastructure and engineered responses, particularly in the context of climate adaptation and mitigation.

Circular design, on the other hand, stems from the principles of the circular economy. It aims to move beyond the linear "take-make-dispose" model by designing products, systems, and processes that minimize waste, extend the useful life of materials, and enable continuous regeneration. In the context of environmental planning and infrastructure development, circular design involves closed-loop systems where resources such as water, nutrients, and materials are reused or recycled, reducing the overall environmental footprint.

The conceptual overlap between NBS and circular design lies in their shared commitment to regeneration and efficiency. NBS contribute to circularity by maintaining and enhancing the natural cycles that sustain ecosystems. For instance, wetlands used for water purification not only provide habitat but also function as self-sustaining filtration systems that reduce the need for energy-intensive treatment plants. Similarly, green roofs and urban forests help manage stormwater while capturing carbon and moderating urban temperatures, aligning with circular principles of resource cycling and multifunctionality.

Moreover, both approaches are inherently adaptive and context-specific. They emphasize locally appropriate solutions that are flexible and resilient in the face of changing environmental and societal conditions. This adaptability makes them well-suited to addressing complex, interdependent challenges such as urbanization, land degradation, and climate change.

Integrating NBS and circular design can lead to synergistic outcomes that enhance both ecological performance and human well-being. By designing with natural systems in mind, planners, engineers, and policymakers can create regenerative infrastructure that not only minimizes harm but actively restores degraded ecosystems. In doing so, these integrated strategies also support biodiversity conservation, improve social equity, and generate economic opportunities linked to sustainable practices.

This section sets the stage for the deeper exploration of concepts, strategies, and systems that follows. Subsequent chapters will examine how nature-based and circular principles can be applied across different sectors and geographies to support climate resilience, biodiversity enhancement, and the transition to a more sustainable and inclusive future.

Barriers in Traditional Infrastructure and Linear Models

Traditional infrastructure systems and linear models of development have supported economic growth and urbanization for decades. However, these models are increasingly being recognized as inadequate for addressing the complex environmental and societal challenges of the 21st century. Characterized by centralized, resource-intensive processes and single-function designs, traditional infrastructure often fails to account for ecological dynamics, resource constraints, and climate risks. The limitations of these approaches are particularly evident in sectors such as water management, energy, waste, and land use, where inefficiencies and vulnerabilities have become more pronounced under conditions of environmental stress.

One of the core barriers of traditional infrastructure lies in its linear logic: resources are extracted, processed, consumed, and then discarded as waste. This take-make-dispose model results in significant environmental degradation, including pollution, loss of biodiversity, and greenhouse gas emissions. It also contributes to the depletion of finite resources such as fresh water, fertile soil, and raw materials. Moreover, the reliance on centralized systems—such as large-scale water treatment plants or energy grids—limits flexibility and responsiveness, especially in regions facing rapid urban growth or climate-induced variability.

Another key limitation is the focus on single-functionality. Traditional infrastructure is typically designed to perform one task—such as flood control, transportation, or waste disposal—without considering opportunities for multifunctional integration. This narrow design philosophy often leads to fragmented landscapes, inefficient land use, and missed opportunities for delivering co-benefits. For example, conventional stormwater systems channel runoff away from urban areas but do not contribute to groundwater recharge, cooling, or habitat provision—benefits that could be delivered through more integrated, nature-based approaches.

Institutional and regulatory barriers also contribute to the persistence of linear models. Many infrastructure and planning systems are governed by sector-specific regulations, funding streams, and performance metrics that reinforce siloed approaches. These frameworks can discourage innovation and limit the ability to adopt integrated solutions that span across environmental, social, and economic domains. Additionally, existing procurement and investment models often prioritize short-term cost savings over long-term resilience and ecosystem performance, reducing incentives to invest in regenerative or circular alternatives.

Social and cultural norms further reinforce linear thinking in design and consumption. Public expectations and market behaviors often align with standardized, high-consumption lifestyles that generate large volumes of waste and undervalue natural services. The invisibility of ecosystem functions in economic accounting compounds this problem, as the benefits of nature-based and circular solutions—such as biodiversity support, air purification, and heat mitigation—are rarely reflected in decision-making processes or infrastructure valuations.

Furthermore, traditional infrastructure systems are often ill-equipped to cope with the uncertainties and intensifying impacts of climate change. Fixed, rigid structures can fail under extreme weather conditions, while the absence of redundancy and adaptability limits their effectiveness in dynamic environments. In contrast, nature-based and circular systems offer more flexible, distributed, and adaptive characteristics that are better suited for long-term climate resilience.

Finally, capacity gaps within institutions and professional disciplines can hinder the uptake of integrated solutions. Engineers, urban planners, and policymakers may lack the training, tools, or cross-sectoral experience needed to implement circular design and NBS effectively. This skills mismatch slows the transition toward more sustainable practices and reinforces reliance on conventional methods.

Addressing these barriers requires a fundamental shift in how infrastructure is conceived, designed, financed, and governed. It calls for a systems-based approach that recognizes the interconnectedness of natural and built environments, the value of ecosystem services, and the need for regenerative, resilient solutions. By identifying and understanding the limitations of linear models, stakeholders can better evaluate the opportunities presented by nature-based and circular approaches—an exploration that begins in the next section of this chapter.

Synergies Between NBS and Circular Economy Frameworks

NBS and circular economy frameworks share several foundational principles, including the efficient use of resources, system-wide thinking, and long-term ecological sustainability. When integrated, these approaches offer a powerful means of designing systems that not only reduce environmental impact but also regenerate natural capital. Understanding the synergies between NBS and circular economy thinking is essential for developing holistic strategies that meet the needs of both people and the planet.

At the core of both frameworks is the concept of working with, rather than against, natural systems. NBS aim to restore and enhance ecological processes to deliver services such as flood control, air purification, climate regulation, and biodiversity protection. Similarly, the circular economy emphasizes the creation of closed-loop systems that emulate natural cycles by minimizing waste and maximizing resource efficiency. When combined, these strategies promote resilience, regeneration, and multifunctionality across sectors and scales.

One area where these synergies are particularly evident is in material and resource management. Circular design encourages the reduction of raw material extraction through reuse, recycling, and regeneration. Nature-based systems inherently support these aims by providing natural processes that facilitate the cycling of water, nutrients, and organic matter. For example, composting organic waste through natural decomposition processes contributes to soil health and fertility, reducing the need for synthetic fertilizers and enhancing carbon sequestration. Wetlands, forests, and other ecosystems similarly process and filter nutrients and contaminants, reinforcing the idea that nature can serve as a processing agent within circular flows.

Water management is another domain in which the integration of NBS and circular principles produces strong synergies. Traditional water infrastructure systems are typically linear—drawing water from a source, treating it, distributing it for use, and disposing of it after use. By contrast, nature-based and circular approaches emphasize reuse, retention, and infiltration. Rain gardens, bioswales, green roofs, and permeable surfaces all help manage stormwater in ways that mimic natural hydrological cycles, reduce runoff, and replenish groundwater. At the same time, circular design ensures that water is used efficiently, treated at the point of use where feasible, and returned to the environment in a safe and useful form.

Synergies are also present in the design of urban green infrastructure. Green spaces, tree-lined streets, and vegetated corridors contribute to climate adaptation and human well-being by reducing the urban heat island effect, improving air quality, and providing recreational areas. When informed by circular thinking, these interventions can be designed to include modular, reusable components, such as prefabricated planters made from recycled materials, or adaptive soil systems that can be relocated or upgraded as conditions change. Such designs align ecological benefits with material circularity, offering both environmental and operational advantages.

In the energy sector, the circular economy seeks to reduce dependence on fossil fuels through renewable energy and the recovery of waste heat and bioenergy. NBS complement these efforts by contributing to energy demand reduction. For example, green walls and roofs improve building insulation, reducing the need for heating and cooling. Moreover, biomass from managed ecosystems can be used in closed-loop energy systems where organic waste is converted to energy and nutrient-rich by-products are returned to the land.

The integration of NBS and circular design also supports the transition to a regenerative economy—one that not only minimizes harm but actively restores ecosystems and communities. While the traditional sustainability paradigm focuses on reducing negative impacts, regenerative design seeks to create net-positive outcomes. Nature-based circular systems can support this ambition by enhancing soil health, restoring watersheds, and creating multifunctional landscapes that support biodiversity, sequester carbon, and deliver social benefits. These systems can also generate livelihoods through activities such as agroforestry, ecological restoration, and sustainable construction, promoting a more inclusive form of economic development.

Moreover, circularity enhances the functionality and durability of NBS by ensuring that materials used in implementation—such as construction components for wetlands, urban forests, or eco-friendly drainage—are sustainable, non-toxic, and easily repurposed or recycled at the end of their service life. This integration improves the environmental performance of NBS while aligning them with the goals of reducing embodied emissions and material extraction.

A further area of synergy lies in the measurement and valuation of benefits. Both frameworks emphasize the importance of understanding long-term outcomes and system-level performance. Circular metrics—such as resource productivity, waste reduction, and material efficiency—can complement NBS indicators such as ecosystem service valuation, biodiversity gains, and climate adaptation outcomes. Together, these metrics enable more comprehensive assessments of environmental performance and support the case for integrated planning and investment.

Institutional frameworks and governance systems also benefit from a dual focus on NBS and circularity. Cross-sectoral coordination, participatory planning, and co-design are key elements of both approaches, ensuring that interventions are socially acceptable, economically viable, and ecologically sound. Incorporating circular principles into NBS policy frameworks encourages long-term thinking, innovation, and adaptive management, while NBS principles strengthen the ecological basis of circular economy initiatives.

Finally, integrating circular economy thinking into NBS planning can help overcome barriers to mainstreaming by aligning ecological goals with economic incentives. By demonstrating cost savings, efficiency gains, and reduced dependence on external inputs, circular NBS projects can appeal to a wider range of stakeholders, including private sector actors, utilities, and local governments. The co-benefits generated through this integration—such as improved public health, job creation, and environmental stewardship—further reinforce the value proposition of these solutions.

In summary, NBS and circular economy frameworks are deeply interconnected. By leveraging the strengths of both, it is possible to design systems that are not only efficient and low-impact but also regenerative and resilient. The combined approach offers a strategic pathway for addressing environmental challenges at multiple scales, delivering outcomes that support ecological integrity, human well-being, and long-term sustainability. The following chapters explore these themes in more depth, with applications in climate mitigation, adaptation, biodiversity, governance, finance, and equity.

How Integration Can Drive Long-Term Resilience

Integrating NBS with circular design offers a strategic opportunity to build long-term resilience across environmental, social, and economic systems. This integration enhances the ability of communities, ecosystems, and infrastructure to anticipate, absorb, and adapt to changing conditions, particularly those associated with climate change, biodiversity loss, and resource scarcity. By aligning ecological functions with resource efficiency, integrated approaches reduce systemic vulnerabilities while supporting regeneration and sustainability.

Resilience, in this context, is not only about the capacity to recover from disturbances but also about the ability to evolve in response to emerging risks and opportunities. Traditional approaches to infrastructure and planning often rely on fixed, centralized systems that can be brittle in the face of disruptions. In contrast, integrated NBS and circular systems are decentralized, adaptive, and multifunctional, enabling them to provide continuous benefits under a range of conditions. For example, green infrastructure that absorbs stormwater also provides cooling during heatwaves and habitat for urban biodiversity, delivering overlapping layers of resilience.

Circular design enhances the durability and adaptability of NBS by supporting closed-loop material and energy flows. This reduces dependence on finite resources and external inputs while minimizing waste and emissions. Over time, such systems require fewer interventions and lower maintenance costs, contributing to financial resilience and long-term performance. When materials and energy are sourced sustainably and cycled effectively, the environmental footprint of NBS is minimized, and their contribution to broader sustainability goals is maximized.

Integrated approaches also support social resilience by providing equitable access to ecosystem services and involving communities in planning and stewardship. Co-designed NBS, when informed by circular principles, can address social and environmental vulnerabilities simultaneously—for instance, by improving local air quality, creating green jobs, and reducing exposure to urban heat and flooding in underserved areas. This fosters trust, participation, and capacity-building, which are key components of resilience at the community level.

Ecologically, the integration of NBS and circular design promotes the restoration and maintenance of ecosystem functions that are essential for long-term adaptability. Healthy ecosystems are better able to withstand and recover from shocks such as droughts, floods, and pest outbreaks. Circularity reinforces this by designing systems that avoid overexploitation and instead replenish natural capital— such as maintaining soil fertility through organic nutrient cycles or preserving water flows through decentralized reuse systems.

In governance terms, the integration of these approaches encourages cross-sectoral coordination and long-term thinking. Planning frameworks that embed both nature-based and circular principles help break down institutional silos and align policies with sustainability and resilience objectives. Such alignment is crucial for responding to complex, interconnected risks and for scaling up solutions across different contexts and geographies.

In sum, the integration of NBS and circular design is a forward-looking strategy that strengthens resilience by addressing root causes of vulnerability and enabling regenerative cycles of growth and adaptation. As the pressures of climate change and ecological degradation intensify, this combined approach offers a robust foundation for sustainable development and systemic transformation.

Chapter 2: Regenerative Urban and Landscape Planning

This chapter explores how NBS and circular design principles can be applied to urban and landscape planning in ways that regenerate ecological function and enhance long-term resilience. As cities expand and landscapes become increasingly fragmented, planning approaches that restore natural processes and close resource loops are gaining relevance.

Regenerative planning moves beyond minimizing environmental impacts to actively improving ecosystem health, connectivity, and multifunctionality. By integrating NBS and circular strategies into spatial planning, urban environments and broader landscapes can be designed to manage water, reduce heat, support biodiversity, and foster inclusive, liveable spaces.

The chapter examines the challenges of traditional infrastructure and land-use models, outlines the benefits of regenerative systems, and presents key considerations for incorporating circularity into urban and regional planning frameworks. It provides a foundation for understanding how design at the landscape scale can deliver environmental, social, and economic co-benefits.

Urban Ecosystems As Regenerative Assets

Urban ecosystems play a vital role in shaping the sustainability and resilience of cities. As concentrations of population, infrastructure, and economic activity continue to grow, urban areas face increasing environmental pressures, including heat stress, poor air and water quality, biodiversity loss, and vulnerability to climate-related hazards. In this context, urban ecosystems are increasingly recognized not only as green spaces or aesthetic features but as critical regenerative assets that contribute to long-term environmental and social well-being.

A regenerative approach views urban ecosystems as active components of urban infrastructure that deliver essential services such as carbon sequestration, temperature regulation, water management, and habitat provision. Unlike traditional grey infrastructure, which typically offers a single function and often disrupts ecological processes, regenerative systems are designed to work in harmony with natural cycles. This perspective encourages a shift in how cities are planned, built, and maintained—placing ecological functionality and resilience at the core of urban development.

Green spaces, such as parks, urban forests, wetlands, and green roofs, exemplify how natural elements can be integrated into the urban fabric to provide multiple benefits. These systems not only enhance biodiversity within densely populated environments but also contribute to human health, well-being, and social cohesion. When strategically designed, urban ecosystems can form interconnected networks that improve ecological connectivity and enable species movement across fragmented landscapes. This connectivity is essential for maintaining ecosystem health and supporting adaptive responses to environmental change.

Urban ecosystems also play a role in the circular management of resources. For example, decentralized green infrastructure can support stormwater retention and infiltration, reducing pressure on drainage systems and replenishing groundwater. Composting organic waste from households and food establishments can be used to enrich soils in urban gardens, closing nutrient loops and reducing the need for synthetic inputs. These functions highlight the compatibility between regenerative urban ecosystems and circular economy principles, where waste is minimized and resources are cycled back into productive use.

Moreover, framing urban ecosystems as regenerative assets shifts the focus from mitigation and maintenance to renewal and improvement. This approach emphasizes restoring degraded spaces, enhancing ecological function, and designing for future adaptability. It also supports long-term cost efficiency by reducing reliance on energy-intensive services and infrastructure, while improving resilience to climate-related shocks such as flooding and extreme heat events.

Recognizing the value of urban ecosystems requires a redefinition of infrastructure to include natural and semi-natural systems alongside conventional built structures. It also demands an integrated planning process that considers environmental, social, and economic factors collectively. Urban planners, architects, engineers, and policymakers all have roles to play in embedding regenerative thinking into city design and management.

In conclusion, urban ecosystems should be viewed not as passive green areas but as dynamic, multifunctional systems capable of regenerating natural capital and enhancing urban resilience. Their integration into the design and operation of cities presents an opportunity to shift toward more sustainable, inclusive, and adaptive urban futures.

Fragmentation, Sprawl, and Design Inefficiencies

Urban expansion over the past century has often followed patterns characterized by fragmentation, low-density sprawl, and design inefficiencies. These development trends have led to a range of environmental, social, and economic challenges that compromise the ability of cities to operate sustainably and adapt to changing conditions. Understanding the systemic barriers created by these patterns is critical for rethinking how cities can integrate nature-based and circular design approaches to support regenerative outcomes.

Fragmentation refers to the division of land into disconnected and isolated parcels, often resulting from uncoordinated development and infrastructure planning. This process can disrupt ecological networks, reducing habitat availability and impairing ecosystem functions. In urban environments, fragmented green spaces are typically surrounded by impermeable surfaces, limiting the movement of species, interrupting water infiltration, and contributing to localized heat accumulation. From a planning perspective, fragmentation makes it more difficult to implement cohesive green infrastructure strategies, as isolated patches provide fewer cumulative benefits than well-connected systems.

Urban sprawl compounds these challenges by extending development over large areas with low population densities. Sprawl often leads to the consumption of agricultural land and natural habitats, increasing land-use pressures and vehicle dependency. As cities spread outward, the costs of providing services such as transportation, water, and energy rise, and reliance on private vehicles increases greenhouse gas emissions and air pollution. Sprawl also contributes to the social segregation of urban areas, as infrastructure and services are unequally distributed, reinforcing disparities in access to environmental amenities and economic opportunities.

Design inefficiencies in the built environment further exacerbate the impacts of fragmentation and sprawl. Many conventional developments prioritize vehicle traffic, impermeable surfaces, and single-use zoning over mixed-use, walkable, and ecologically integrated designs. Streets and rooftops are often impervious to water, leading to excessive runoff, flooding, and pollution of water bodies. Buildings are frequently constructed without regard for passive solar design, natural ventilation, or local climatic conditions, increasing energy demand for heating and cooling.

From a systems perspective, these inefficiencies reflect a lack of circular thinking in urban design. Resources flow linearly through cities—from extraction and consumption to disposal—without efforts to recapture value or reduce waste. Green spaces are frequently underutilized in terms of ecosystem service delivery, and construction practices often rely on virgin materials rather than renewable, recycled, or modular alternatives. Opportunities to integrate nature-based elements into streetscapes, buildings, and public spaces are commonly overlooked, resulting in designs that underperform in terms of climate resilience, biodiversity support, and social well-being.

These patterns are reinforced by planning and governance frameworks that prioritize short-term economic returns over long-term environmental performance. Land-use regulations may encourage expansive development rather than compact, transit-oriented growth. Infrastructure investments often favor grey solutions over green or hybrid alternatives. Meanwhile, limited coordination between sectors and jurisdictions hampers efforts to plan holistically or integrate nature-based and circular strategies at scale.

Reversing these trends requires a shift toward more compact, connected, and multifunctional urban forms. This includes prioritizing infill development, retrofitting existing spaces, and enhancing connectivity between green areas to support ecological and social functions. It also involves embedding circular principles in design processes to reduce resource consumption, eliminate waste, and optimize performance across building lifecycles and infrastructure systems.

By addressing the underlying inefficiencies of fragmented and sprawling urban development, cities can lay the foundation for regenerative transformation. Integrating NBS and circular design practices offers a pathway to more efficient, equitable, and resilient urban environments capable of meeting the demands of the future.

Circular Design Strategies for Regenerative Cities

Circular design offers a structured approach to transforming cities into regenerative systems that reduce environmental impacts, close resource loops, and enhance ecological and social resilience. As cities face growing pressures from population growth, climate change, and resource scarcity, circular design principles provide a practical and adaptable framework for rethinking urban form, function, and infrastructure. These principles can be applied across scales—from individual buildings and neighborhoods to metropolitan regions—to create cities that regenerate rather than deplete natural and human capital.

At the core of circular design is the idea of maintaining the value of resources for as long as possible by designing out waste and pollution, keeping materials in use, and regenerating natural systems. In an urban context, this translates into design strategies that support multifunctionality, adaptability, and circular material flows. These strategies are not only aligned with sustainability goals but also serve to embed resilience into the built environment by reducing reliance on finite resources and enhancing the capacity of urban systems to respond to shocks and stressors.

One fundamental strategy involves designing buildings and infrastructure for longevity, flexibility, and reuse. This includes the use of modular construction techniques, reversible joints, and standardized components that can be easily disassembled and repurposed. Materials with high durability and low embodied carbon are prioritized, and buildings are constructed to accommodate different functions over time. This design for adaptability supports changing user needs and reduces the frequency and impact of demolition and reconstruction, thereby lowering material consumption and waste generation.

Material circularity is also a central component of regenerative urban design. This involves sourcing construction materials that are renewable, recyclable, or locally available to minimize transport emissions and ecological impact. Urban mining—recovering materials from existing buildings and infrastructure—can be employed to reduce dependence on virgin resources. Additionally, material passports and digital building logbooks can support tracking and reuse by documenting material origins, composition, and lifecycle performance.

In public infrastructure and urban spaces, circular design encourages multifunctional systems that deliver environmental, social, and economic co-benefits. For example, a linear park may function simultaneously as a stormwater buffer, recreational area, biodiversity corridor, and non-motorized transport route. Integrating NBS into circular design further amplifies these benefits by incorporating processes such as infiltration, shading, carbon sequestration, and pollination. By optimizing land use and infrastructure performance through multifunctionality, cities can reduce costs and improve outcomes across sectors.

Water-sensitive urban design (WSUD) is another key example of circularity in action. This approach manages the urban water cycle in a closed loop, emphasizing rainwater harvesting, greywater reuse, and decentralized treatment systems. Green roofs, permeable pavements, and constructed wetlands work in concert to reduce runoff, improve water quality, and support groundwater recharge. These systems are designed to function dynamically and restore natural hydrological patterns within the urban landscape.

Energy systems can also be designed for circularity by integrating renewable energy sources, capturing waste heat, and enabling decentralized production and storage. In regenerative cities, buildings become energy producers as well as consumers through rooftop solar installations, passive design, and demand-side management. At the district scale, microgrids and energy-sharing platforms promote efficiency, resilience, and local control.

Food systems represent another opportunity for circular design. Urban agriculture, composting, and food waste valorization can be incorporated into city planning to create closed nutrient loops and reduce organic waste. By reconnecting food production with consumption areas, cities can lower emissions, shorten supply chains, and foster local food security. Composted organic waste can be returned to urban soils or peri-urban farms to improve soil health and support ecosystem services.

Mobility systems designed according to circular principles prioritize shared, low-impact, and low-resource options. Compact, walkable neighborhoods with mixed land use reduce the need for motorized travel and support active transport. Shared mobility platforms, electric public transport, and cycling infrastructure contribute to lower emissions and resource use while improving accessibility and public health. Integrating transport planning with green infrastructure and circular land use strategies enhances connectivity and reduces environmental burdens.

Digitally enabled circularity is an emerging domain with significant potential. Digital twins, smart sensors, and data platforms can optimize resource flows, monitor environmental conditions, and inform adaptive management. These tools support predictive maintenance, real-time performance tracking, and community engagement in sustainability initiatives. Digital integration also enables more transparent decision-making and facilitates collaboration across stakeholders.

Governance plays a key role in scaling circular design strategies. Urban policies and planning frameworks must align with circular principles by encouraging lifecycle thinking, cross-sector coordination, and participatory processes. Regulatory tools such as green building standards, zoning incentives, and procurement criteria can drive adoption of circular approaches. Financial mechanisms, including circular investment funds and outcome-based financing, can support innovation and de-risk projects with longer payback periods.

Capacity-building and education are equally important to ensure that circular design becomes embedded in urban practice. Training programs, research partnerships, and demonstration projects can promote knowledge sharing and foster innovation. Professional disciplines—including architecture, engineering, urban planning, and landscape design—must be equipped with tools and methodologies that support regenerative thinking and systems-based approaches.

Ultimately, circular design strategies contribute to regenerative cities by creating conditions in which people and ecosystems can thrive over the long term. These strategies support decoupling economic activity from resource use and environmental harm, while enabling flexibility, adaptability, and innovation. When implemented alongside NBS, circular design becomes a powerful instrument for transforming urban systems into resilient, low-carbon, and biodiverse environments.

Benefits of NBS in Climate-Responsive Spatial Planning

NBS are increasingly recognized as essential components of climate-responsive spatial planning. By integrating natural systems into the built environment, NBS enhance the adaptive capacity of cities and regions while delivering co-benefits across ecological, social, and economic dimensions. Their strategic incorporation into spatial planning processes allows for the design of urban and peri-urban areas that are more resilient to climate variability, reduce emissions, and improve overall quality of life.

One of the key benefits of NBS in spatial planning is their ability to moderate local climate conditions. Urban areas are often subject to the urban heat island effect, where the prevalence of heat-absorbing surfaces and lack of vegetation lead to elevated temperatures. Green infrastructure elements such as trees, parks, green roofs, and vegetated corridors can significantly reduce surface and air temperatures through shading and evapotranspiration. These interventions contribute to thermal comfort, reduce energy demand for cooling, and improve public health outcomes, particularly during heatwaves.

NBS also enhance urban flood resilience by improving the capacity of landscapes to absorb and manage water. Traditional drainage systems are often overwhelmed by increased precipitation due to climate change, leading to surface flooding and water quality degradation. Green spaces, permeable surfaces, bioswales, and constructed wetlands can slow, store, and filter stormwater, reducing runoff volumes and peak flows. By mimicking natural hydrological processes, these features decrease reliance on engineered solutions while restoring ecological functions.

Biodiversity is another area where NBS offer substantial benefits within spatial planning frameworks. The incorporation of green and blue infrastructure creates habitats and ecological corridors that support a variety of species. This connectivity is vital for maintaining ecosystem resilience and enabling species to migrate and adapt in response to changing climatic conditions. Moreover, diverse and healthy ecosystems are better equipped to provide services such as pollination, air purification, and carbon sequestration.

Social benefits are equally important. Accessible green spaces improve mental and physical well-being, promote social cohesion, and provide opportunities for recreation and environmental education. These outcomes are particularly valuable in densely populated urban areas where access to nature is limited. Through inclusive planning and participatory design, NBS can be tailored to meet community needs and contribute to more equitable urban development.

Economically, NBS can offer cost-effective alternatives or complements to conventional infrastructure. While initial investments may be comparable, the long-term operational and maintenance costs of green infrastructure are often lower. Additionally, the multifunctionality of NBS can reduce the need for multiple single-purpose investments, enhancing cost-efficiency. Spatial planning that incorporates NBS can also enhance property values, attract investment, and support local employment in design, maintenance, and stewardship roles.

In summary, integrating NBS into climate-responsive spatial planning offers a range of benefits that align with long-term sustainability and resilience objectives. These solutions support the creation of adaptable urban environments that respond dynamically to climate risks while enhancing ecological integrity and human well-being. As planning systems evolve to meet the demands of a changing climate, NBS will play an increasingly central role in shaping the structure and function of resilient cities.

Chapter 3: Enhancing Biodiversity through Circular Ecosystem Design

This chapter examines how circular design principles can support biodiversity conservation and ecosystem regeneration. As biodiversity loss accelerates due to land-use change, pollution, and resource extraction, there is an urgent need for approaches that not only reduce harm but actively restore ecological integrity.

Circular ecosystem design focuses on creating closed-loop systems that mimic natural cycles, reduce environmental pressures, and enhance habitat quality. When applied thoughtfully, these approaches can strengthen ecological networks, support species diversity, and build ecosystem resilience.

The chapter outlines the drivers of biodiversity loss in linear systems and explores how circular strategies—such as material reuse, soil regeneration, and habitat integration—can contribute to the recovery and long-term viability of ecosystems. It highlights the role of biodiversity as both a beneficiary and enabler of regenerative systems.

Biodiversity Loss and Habitat Degradation

Biodiversity loss and habitat degradation represent critical environmental challenges with far-reaching consequences for ecosystem stability, climate resilience, and human well-being. The degradation of natural habitats due to land-use change, pollution, resource extraction, and infrastructure expansion has led to a marked decline in species richness and ecosystem function across the globe. In urban and peri-urban contexts, these pressures are particularly acute, as built environments continue to expand at the expense of natural and semi-natural landscapes.

Habitat degradation occurs when ecosystems are altered in ways that reduce their ability to support native species and ecological processes. This may involve the fragmentation of landscapes, the introduction of invasive species, pollution from urban runoff, or hydrological changes that affect wetlands and waterways. As habitats become degraded, the structural complexity and quality of ecological niches diminish, resulting in population declines and reduced ecosystem services.

One of the principal drivers of biodiversity loss is land-use conversion, especially for agriculture, infrastructure, and urban development. The transformation of forests, wetlands, grasslands, and other ecosystems into impervious surfaces or monocultural landscapes significantly reduces the availability of habitat for native flora and fauna. These changes not only disrupt species' life cycles and migration routes but also weaken ecosystem interactions such as pollination, seed dispersal, and nutrient cycling.

In cities and rapidly developing regions, habitat degradation is often intensified by the cumulative impacts of multiple stressors. Air and water pollution, noise, light disturbances, and increased human activity contribute to the unsuitability of urban areas for many species. Even in areas where green spaces exist, poor design or management practices—such as the use of non-native plant species or excessive maintenance—can further limit ecological value.

Biodiversity loss has significant implications for the resilience and functionality of ecosystems. Diverse biological communities are generally more stable and better able to adapt to environmental fluctuations, including those driven by climate change. Loss of species can lead to reduced redundancy in ecosystem roles, making systems more vulnerable to disturbance and less capable of recovering from shocks. In turn, the decline in ecosystem services—such as air purification, temperature regulation, water filtration, and food provision—can negatively impact human health and livelihoods.

Furthermore, the erosion of biodiversity undermines opportunities for NBS that rely on healthy ecosystems. Many NBS—such as urban forests, riparian buffers, or restored wetlands—depend on biological diversity to function effectively and deliver multiple co-benefits. When biodiversity is diminished, the capacity of these systems to contribute to climate mitigation, adaptation, and circular resource flows is compromised.

Addressing biodiversity loss and habitat degradation requires integrated responses that prioritize ecological integrity alongside human development needs. This includes safeguarding remaining natural areas, restoring degraded habitats, and embedding biodiversity considerations into spatial planning and infrastructure design. By reversing habitat degradation and promoting species diversity, it is possible to enhance the performance of nature-based and circular systems, supporting both environmental and societal resilience.

Systemic Threats from Extraction and Waste

Resource extraction and waste generation are central features of today's global economic systems. Together, they contribute significantly to environmental degradation, including biodiversity loss, habitat destruction, and pollution. The impacts are often systemic, affecting entire ecosystems through interconnected pressures on land, water, and atmospheric systems. As societies continue to grow and urbanize, the scale and intensity of resource use have exceeded many ecological thresholds, threatening the long-term stability of natural systems and reducing the capacity for regeneration.

Extraction activities, such as mining, logging, agriculture, and infrastructure development, are a major cause of habitat fragmentation and ecosystem disruption. These activities often involve the removal of vegetation, alteration of landforms, and disturbance of soil and water systems. As natural landscapes are cleared or converted for extractive purposes, habitat quality declines and species are displaced, leading to reduced biodiversity and compromised ecosystem functions.

Beyond the immediate effects of land-use change, extraction also contributes to cumulative pressures that alter natural cycles. For example, the removal of topsoil and vegetation disrupts nutrient and hydrological processes, while emissions from fossil fuel extraction contribute to climate change, further stressing ecological systems. Additionally, extractive industries frequently require large volumes of water and energy, placing further demands on local resources and potentially leading to conflicts over access and allocation.

Waste generation is a parallel and reinforcing threat. In linear economic systems, materials are used once and discarded, often without consideration of long-term environmental consequences. The accumulation of waste—particularly plastic, electronic, and construction waste—can have direct and indirect impacts on ecosystems. Improper disposal of waste leads to soil and water contamination, harming terrestrial and aquatic organisms. In urban areas, unmanaged waste contributes to blocked drainage systems, exacerbating flood risks and degrading living conditions.

Organic waste, when not properly managed, generates methane—a potent greenhouse gas—and attracts pests that can spread disease. In many cities, food and green waste are underutilized resources that are landfilled or incinerated rather than composted or reused. This not only represents a missed opportunity for nutrient recovery and soil enhancement but also contributes to emissions and land degradation.

The combined impacts of extraction and waste extend across supply chains and geographic boundaries. High levels of consumption in urban areas often drive resource extraction in rural and remote regions, leading to ecological degradation far from the point of consumption. Similarly, waste exported from one jurisdiction may contribute to pollution and public health challenges elsewhere. These transboundary dynamics make it difficult to manage impacts at a local level and require integrated, systems-based approaches.

From a biodiversity perspective, the effects of extraction and waste are particularly severe. Many species are sensitive to changes in land cover, water quality, and food availability—all of which are affected by extractive activities and waste accumulation. Pollutants such as heavy metals, microplastics, and persistent organic compounds can accumulate in food chains, impair reproductive health, and reduce population viability. For threatened and endangered species, these additional pressures can be decisive.

Addressing these systemic threats requires a shift from linear, extractive economic models toward regenerative and circular systems that reduce demand for raw materials and minimize waste. NBS play a critical role by restoring degraded ecosystems, filtering pollutants, and supporting closed-loop resource flows. When combined with circular design strategies that prioritize reuse, recycling, and material recovery, NBS can help reduce the ecological footprint of human activity and create more sustainable relationships between society and nature.

Circular Designs That Support Species and Ecosystems

Circular design provides a framework for reducing environmental degradation while actively supporting species conservation and ecosystem health. By mimicking natural cycles and minimizing resource extraction and waste, circular systems can be structured to align with the ecological requirements of biodiversity. This approach goes beyond minimizing harm and instead emphasizes regeneration, resilience, and interdependence between built environments and natural systems. In doing so, circular design serves as a foundation for integrating biodiversity goals into infrastructure, land use, and product systems.

Fundamentally, circular design seeks to close material, water, and energy loops. In this process, natural systems are viewed not as externalities, but as integral components of a functioning economy. Supporting biodiversity within a circular framework means designing environments that promote habitat continuity, minimize pollutants, and integrate natural processes that benefit multiple species. These design practices create synergies between ecological and human systems, providing long-term sustainability and resilience benefits.

One of the key strategies for supporting biodiversity in circular design is the restoration and protection of habitat within and adjacent to human settlements. Green infrastructure—including green roofs, green walls, bioswales, and urban forests—can be planned and managed to provide essential resources for pollinators, birds, and small mammals. The inclusion of native plant species, diverse vegetation structures, and minimal chemical inputs supports species richness and ecosystem stability. Green corridors that connect fragmented patches allow for species movement and genetic exchange, both of which are critical for long-term viability of wildlife populations.

Circular design also emphasizes multifunctionality, where infrastructure and public spaces deliver ecological as well as social and economic benefits. For instance, water-sensitive urban design features such as retention ponds, rain gardens, and permeable pavements can simultaneously manage stormwater and provide aquatic and terrestrial habitat. These systems replicate natural hydrological cycles, supporting amphibians, insects, and vegetation while improving water quality. Similarly, urban agriculture projects designed with circular principles can incorporate pollinator-friendly plants and compost-based soil regeneration, contributing to biodiversity while reducing food system impacts.

In the context of buildings and materials, circular strategies can support biodiversity through responsible sourcing, low-impact material selection, and end-of-life reuse. Using bio-based materials such as timber from certified sustainable forestry, mycelium-based composites, or recycled construction waste helps reduce the footprint of built environments. Designs that reduce artificial lighting at night, mitigate heat island effects, and incorporate bird-safe glass can further reduce impacts on urban wildlife. Lifecycle assessments can

31

be used to evaluate and optimize material choices to ensure compatibility with biodiversity objectives.

Designing for circularity also includes managing organic waste in ways that restore ecosystems. Composting and anaerobic digestion convert organic matter into nutrient-rich inputs that can be returned to soils, enhancing soil biodiversity and fertility. This improves the conditions for native vegetation and supports food webs at multiple levels. Compost can be applied in parks, gardens, reforestation sites, and degraded lands to enhance moisture retention and microbial diversity, which are essential for healthy ecosystems.

Water reuse systems can be designed to maintain flow regimes in natural waterways, benefiting aquatic habitats and dependent species. Greywater and rainwater harvesting systems that return treated water to the landscape can reduce stress on urban rivers and groundwater reserves. When implemented alongside riparian buffers or constructed wetlands, these systems provide habitat while contributing to circular water management and climate adaptation objectives.

In the agricultural landscape, circular approaches such as agroecology and agroforestry promote practices that enhance biodiversity while maintaining productivity. These include crop rotation, polycultures, habitat strips, and soil conservation measures that increase ecosystem complexity and support beneficial species. By minimizing chemical inputs and preserving natural habitat features, such systems maintain ecological functions while providing food and raw materials in closed-loop cycles.

Industrial systems can also be redesigned using principles of industrial ecology, where the by-products of one process serve as inputs for another. Eco-industrial parks are an example of this approach, where co-location of businesses enables the exchange of energy, materials, and water. When planned with ecological considerations, such parks can incorporate green spaces, stormwater management, and biodiversity-friendly landscaping. These features contribute to urban greening and enhance ecological performance in areas typically dominated by grey infrastructure.

Digital technologies and data analytics further support circular design for biodiversity by enabling real-time monitoring and adaptive management. Geographic information systems (GIS), remote sensing, and environmental sensors can track changes in land cover, species presence, and environmental quality. This information can guide maintenance practices, optimize ecological outcomes, and ensure that circular systems are functioning as intended. Data-driven decision-making also helps build accountability and improve performance over time.

Governance and policy frameworks have an important role in mainstreaming circular design for biodiversity. Planning codes, building regulations, and procurement guidelines can set standards for habitat provision, material reuse, and lifecycle impacts. Incentives such as green infrastructure grants, biodiversity credits, and circular economy funds can support investment in integrated projects. Interdepartmental coordination across planning, environment, transport, and housing authorities can facilitate the implementation of circular strategies that deliver biodiversity benefits at scale.

Public engagement and education are also critical components. Involving communities in the design, implementation, and stewardship of circular systems helps build ecological awareness and encourages practices that support biodiversity. Citizen science initiatives, community gardens, and local conservation programs create opportunities for residents to contribute to environmental protection while benefiting from greener, more livable neighborhoods.

In summary, circular design provides a pathway for embedding biodiversity support into the fabric of cities, infrastructure, and production systems. Through multifunctionality, resource cycling, and habitat integration, circular approaches contribute to ecological regeneration and the creation of resilient socio-ecological systems. When designed with biodiversity in mind, circular systems not only reduce negative impacts but actively enhance the conditions necessary for diverse species and healthy ecosystems to thrive.

Biodiversity as a Feedback Loop in NBS

Biodiversity functions not only as a desired outcome of NBS but also as a key component of their effectiveness and long-term resilience. In well-designed NBS, biodiversity and ecosystem health form a feedback loop—enhanced biodiversity strengthens ecological processes, which in turn reinforces the performance and sustainability of the solution itself. Recognizing this interdependence is critical for designing interventions that are both ecologically robust and adaptive to future environmental conditions.

Healthy ecosystems typically exhibit high levels of functional and species diversity, which increases their capacity to deliver multiple ecosystem services. In NBS, this includes services such as water purification, flood regulation, carbon sequestration, pollination, and temperature moderation. The presence of diverse plant and animal species contributes to the stability and resilience of these services, especially under conditions of environmental stress or disturbance. Functional diversity ensures that different species can compensate for one another if specific populations decline, thereby sustaining ecological functions over time.

For example, in wetland restoration projects, a diverse assemblage of plant species can improve water filtration capacity, support a wider range of aquatic and terrestrial life, and provide greater resilience to invasive species or hydrological changes. Similarly, urban green spaces with high plant diversity tend to attract a broader range of pollinators, birds, and insects, creating more stable and interconnected ecological communities. These interactions enhance the effectiveness of NBS and contribute to the overall regenerative potential of the landscape.

34

Biodiversity also contributes to soil health, which is foundational for many terrestrial NBS. A diverse soil microbiome enhances nutrient cycling, organic matter breakdown, and plant productivity. In turn, healthy soils support robust vegetation growth, which strengthens erosion control, water retention, and carbon storage. This feedback between biological activity and ecosystem function demonstrates the integral role of biodiversity in maintaining system performance.

The feedback loop can be further strengthened through intentional design that prioritizes ecological integrity. Selecting native species adapted to local conditions helps support existing food webs and avoids unintended disruptions. Incorporating habitat structures— such as ponds, logs, hedgerows, and nesting sites—encourages species colonization and persistence. The ongoing presence of biodiversity not only sustains NBS functionality but also enhances their value for education, recreation, and cultural connection.

Monitoring and adaptive management are essential to maintaining biodiversity as a dynamic component of NBS. Ecosystems are subject to change over time due to external pressures such as climate change, land-use shifts, and species migration. Tracking biodiversity indicators allows practitioners to evaluate the performance of NBS, identify early warning signs of degradation, and adjust management practices accordingly. In this way, biodiversity informs the adaptive capacity of the system and supports continuous improvement.

In conclusion, biodiversity should be understood not simply as a co-benefit of NBS but as a critical enabler of their success. The reciprocal relationship between ecological diversity and system function forms a reinforcing feedback loop that strengthens resilience, enhances multifunctionality, and supports long-term environmental and societal outcomes. Designing for and with biodiversity is therefore essential to unlocking the full potential of NBS.

Chapter 4: Climate Mitigation: Capturing Carbon through Circular Nature

This chapter explores the role of NBS and circular design in supporting climate mitigation through enhanced carbon capture and retention. As global efforts intensify to reduce greenhouse gas emissions, integrating natural systems into mitigation strategies offers an effective and multifunctional pathway to climate stability.

Natural ecosystems—including forests, wetlands, soils, and coastal habitats—function as carbon sinks, absorbing and storing carbon over time. However, these systems are increasingly disrupted by linear development models that degrade landscapes and release stored carbon. Circular approaches that restore and maintain ecosystem functions can reverse these trends by closing carbon loops and enhancing long-term sequestration.

The chapter examines how regenerative practices, material choices, and integrated land-use strategies contribute to carbon mitigation while delivering additional environmental and social benefits. It highlights the potential of circular nature systems to serve as a foundation for resilient, low-carbon development.

Ecosystems as Carbon Sinks

Ecosystems serve as natural carbon sinks by capturing and storing atmospheric carbon dioxide through biological processes. This role is essential in global efforts to mitigate climate change, as terrestrial and aquatic ecosystems contribute significantly to the removal of greenhouse gases from the atmosphere. Forests, wetlands, grasslands, soils, and marine systems absorb carbon through photosynthesis and sequester it in biomass and sediments over varying timescales. Recognizing and preserving the carbon sink function of ecosystems is critical to achieving net-zero targets and maintaining climate stability.

Forests are among the most effective carbon sinks, storing carbon in both aboveground biomass and belowground root systems. Mature forests accumulate carbon over decades or even centuries, with tropical, temperate, and boreal forests contributing differently depending on their structure and climatic conditions. Afforestation, reforestation, and improved forest management practices can enhance carbon uptake while providing co-benefits such as habitat conservation, soil stabilization, and water regulation. However, deforestation and forest degradation release stored carbon, underscoring the need for protection and sustainable management.

Wetlands, including peatlands, mangroves, and salt marshes, are also highly effective carbon sinks due to their ability to store large amounts of carbon in waterlogged soils and sediments. These systems accumulate organic matter under anaerobic conditions, slowing decomposition and enabling long-term carbon storage. Peatlands, despite covering a relatively small portion of the Earth's surface, store more carbon than all the world's forests combined. Disturbance or drainage of these ecosystems, however, can rapidly reverse their carbon sink function, releasing significant emissions.

Grasslands and savannas also contribute to carbon sequestration, particularly through root biomass and soil organic carbon. Although their aboveground carbon storage is lower than that of forests, these ecosystems are often more resilient to disturbance and can recover carbon stocks relatively quickly after sustainable management interventions such as rotational grazing or native species restoration. The potential for carbon storage in these systems is often underestimated but remains an important component of broader climate strategies.

Soils represent one of the largest carbon reservoirs, with the capacity to store carbon for hundreds to thousands of years depending on land use and management practices. Agricultural soils, when managed using techniques such as cover cropping, conservation tillage, and organic amendments, can increase their carbon content. Restoring degraded lands and improving soil health not only supports climate mitigation goals but also enhances agricultural productivity and ecosystem resilience.

Aquatic ecosystems, including oceans, seagrass beds, and kelp forests, play a complementary role in carbon sequestration. Known as "blue carbon" systems, these environments capture carbon in both plant biomass and ocean sediments. Coastal ecosystems, in particular, offer high rates of carbon uptake per unit area and provide important buffering functions against sea-level rise and storm surges. Their preservation and restoration are increasingly recognized in climate policy and planning frameworks.

Overall, the role of ecosystems as carbon sinks illustrates the importance of conserving and enhancing natural systems as part of climate mitigation efforts. Integrating NBS into carbon strategies ensures that emissions reductions are accompanied by biodiversity gains, water regulation, and long-term landscape resilience.

Disrupted Carbon Cycles in Linear Systems

Linear economic and development systems have significantly disrupted the natural carbon cycle, contributing to increased atmospheric carbon dioxide concentrations and accelerating climate change. In natural ecosystems, carbon flows through a balanced cycle of uptake, storage, and release, regulated by processes such as photosynthesis, respiration, decomposition, and sedimentation. However, the dominance of extractive, consumption-driven models has altered these dynamics by introducing high volumes of carbon emissions, degrading carbon sinks, and reducing the system's capacity for long-term storage.

A key feature of linear systems is their reliance on fossil fuel extraction and combustion. The burning of coal, oil, and natural gas for energy and industrial processes releases large quantities of carbon that had been stored underground for millions of years. This input disrupts the balance of the carbon cycle by injecting geologically stored carbon into the active atmosphere-biosphere system at a rate that far exceeds natural absorption capacities. As a result, carbon accumulates in the atmosphere, enhancing the greenhouse effect and driving global temperature increases.

Land-use change associated with linear development also plays a critical role in disrupting carbon flows. Deforestation, urban expansion, and intensive agriculture often result in the removal of vegetation and soil cover that would otherwise absorb and store carbon. The conversion of forests and grasslands to impervious surfaces or monocultural systems eliminates vital carbon sinks and often leads to the release of carbon previously stored in biomass and soils. Furthermore, degraded ecosystems lose their ability to recover carbon stocks, leading to long-term reductions in carbon sequestration potential.

Industrial and construction practices within linear systems further contribute to carbon cycle disruption through material selection, production methods, and end-of-life disposal. The manufacture of steel, cement, and other construction materials is energy-intensive and heavily reliant on fossil fuels. Additionally, these materials often have high embodied carbon, contributing further to emissions throughout their lifecycle. Linear design typically overlooks reuse and recycling opportunities, resulting in emissions-intensive processes and short-lived infrastructure.

Waste generation is another aspect of linear systems that influences carbon flows. Organic waste, when sent to landfills, decomposes anaerobically and produces methane—a greenhouse gas with a global warming potential significantly higher than carbon dioxide. Food waste, green waste, and other biodegradable materials represent not only lost resources but also contribute to elevated emissions. Incineration of waste materials also produces carbon emissions, particularly when involving plastics or other fossil-derived products.

Soil carbon stocks are affected by agricultural practices common in linear systems, such as intensive tillage, monocropping, and heavy chemical input. These practices degrade soil structure, reduce organic matter content, and accelerate carbon loss through erosion and microbial decomposition. Soils that have been heavily degraded can shift from being carbon sinks to sources of emissions, undermining global climate objectives.

Additionally, linear systems often operate with minimal regard for carbon feedbacks and thresholds. Planning decisions, product designs, and land management strategies may fail to account for cumulative carbon impacts or interactions across sectors. This fragmented approach can amplify carbon disruptions across the system and reduce the effectiveness of isolated mitigation measures.

Addressing these disruptions requires a fundamental reorientation of systems toward circularity and ecological integration. Strategies such as renewable energy adoption, NBS, regenerative agriculture, sustainable construction, and resource cycling can help restore balance to the carbon cycle. In particular, embedding circular principles in land-use planning and production systems offers a pathway to reducing emissions while regenerating carbon sinks and enhancing resilience.

By recognizing how linear models interrupt natural carbon flows, decision-makers and practitioners can better identify points of intervention that support climate mitigation. Transitioning away from linear processes toward regenerative, circular approaches is essential for stabilizing atmospheric carbon levels and restoring the capacity of ecosystems to function as effective, long-term carbon sinks.

NBS and Circular Practices for Carbon Retention

NBS and circular practices present a complementary set of approaches for retaining carbon across urban, rural, and natural systems. As the global focus shifts toward achieving net-zero emissions and enhancing climate resilience, the integration of these two frameworks offers a viable and scalable strategy to reduce carbon emissions and enhance the sequestration capacity of ecosystems and built environments. By working with natural processes and closing resource loops, NBS and circular design principles help to minimize carbon losses and stabilize carbon storage over the long term.

NBS contribute to carbon retention primarily through ecosystem restoration, protection, and sustainable management. When ecosystems such as forests, wetlands, grasslands, and coastal zones are conserved or restored, they absorb carbon dioxide from the atmosphere via photosynthesis and store it in plant biomass, soils, and sediments. Unlike conventional carbon reduction methods that often focus solely on emissions avoidance, NBS offer a dual benefit by removing existing carbon while delivering co-benefits related to biodiversity, water regulation, and human well-being.

Afforestation and reforestation are among the most widely recognized NBS for carbon retention. Strategic tree planting and forest restoration on degraded lands help to rebuild biomass stocks and restore ecological functions. However, these efforts must be guided by ecological principles to avoid negative consequences such as monoculture plantations or displacement of other land uses. Selecting native and diverse species, ensuring long-term maintenance, and aligning planting with water availability are critical for maximizing carbon retention and ecological value.

Wetland and peatland restoration also represent high-impact NBS. These ecosystems sequester substantial amounts of carbon in anaerobic conditions that slow decomposition and promote long-term storage in soils and sediments. Drained or degraded wetlands release stored carbon rapidly, making restoration efforts particularly urgent and impactful. Rewetting peatlands and restoring hydrological connectivity are examples of interventions that not only retain existing carbon stocks but also regenerate natural sequestration processes.

In agricultural landscapes, nature-based practices such as agroforestry, cover cropping, and conservation tillage contribute to carbon retention in both biomass and soils. Agroforestry systems integrate trees with crops or livestock, increasing above- and below-ground carbon stocks while enhancing productivity and resilience. Cover crops prevent soil erosion, add organic matter, and support microbial communities essential for carbon storage. These techniques align with circular principles by reducing input reliance, enhancing soil health, and maintaining productive land use within ecological limits.

Circular economy strategies reinforce NBS by minimizing resource inputs, reducing emissions from waste, and extending the useful life of materials. One of the key pathways to carbon retention through circularity is material reuse and recycling. By designing buildings, products, and infrastructure for disassembly and repurposing, circular design reduces the demand for energy- and carbon-intensive virgin materials such as steel and concrete. Lower demand for extraction and processing in turn reduces upstream emissions and keeps embodied carbon within the material cycle.

Built environment interventions can further contribute to carbon retention when combined with NBS. For instance, green roofs and walls, when constructed with bio-based or reused materials, provide carbon sequestration while improving building insulation and reducing energy use. Incorporating vegetation into urban design helps absorb carbon while moderating urban temperatures, reducing the need for mechanical cooling and associated emissions. When designed with lifecycle performance in mind, these features contribute to long-term carbon savings.

Circular organic waste management supports carbon retention through composting and bioenergy production. Instead of landfilling organic waste—which releases methane—composting returns carbon to the soil in a stable form, improving soil structure and long-term fertility. Anaerobic digestion converts organic waste into biogas and digestate, which can serve as renewable energy and organic fertilizer respectively. These processes form part of a closed-loop nutrient cycle that aligns with both NBS and circular economy objectives.

Water systems offer another opportunity for combined circular and nature-based carbon retention. Constructed wetlands, green infrastructure for stormwater management, and decentralized wastewater systems reduce emissions associated with traditional water treatment while supporting carbon storage in plant biomass and soils. Circular water reuse systems reduce energy demand for water extraction and conveyance, contributing to indirect emissions reductions.

Urban planning and spatial development strategies can also leverage NBS and circular practices to maximize carbon retention. Transit-oriented development, compact land use, and integrated green infrastructure reduce transport-related emissions while preserving open spaces for nature-based interventions. Rehabilitating degraded urban areas through greening and retrofitting supports ecosystem restoration and reduces embodied carbon in new construction. Circular urban metabolism—where energy, materials, and nutrients are cycled within cities—further supports emission reductions and the retention of carbon in physical and biological systems.

Digital technologies enhance the effectiveness of both NBS and circular strategies by enabling more precise monitoring, forecasting, and optimization of carbon flows. Remote sensing, GIS, and digital twins can be used to assess carbon storage potential, track ecosystem health, and inform adaptive management. Material tracking systems and carbon accounting tools support transparency and evidence-based decision-making, ensuring that carbon retention goals are met and maintained over time.

Policy frameworks play a critical role in integrating NBS and circular practices into climate action plans. Carbon pricing mechanisms, green public procurement, and performance-based financing can incentivize projects that prioritize long-term carbon retention. At the same time, environmental regulations and land-use planning tools can protect existing carbon sinks and facilitate the implementation of circular design in infrastructure and development.

Ultimately, the combination of NBS and circular practices enhances the capacity of systems to retain carbon by aligning human activities with ecological processes. By reducing emissions at the source, enhancing natural carbon sinks, and designing out waste, these approaches support a transition toward regenerative systems. As climate mitigation efforts intensify, the role of nature and circularity in achieving durable carbon outcomes will become increasingly central to sustainability and resilience agendas.

Maximizing Mitigation via Closed-Loop Nature Systems

Closed-loop nature systems represent a strategic means of maximizing climate change mitigation by enhancing the efficiency and effectiveness of carbon cycling and storage within ecological and human-modified environments. These systems are characterized by the integration of circular resource flows with natural processes, ensuring that energy, materials, nutrients, and carbon are retained and reused rather than lost to the environment. In the context of climate mitigation, closed-loop systems reduce greenhouse gas emissions at the source, increase carbon sequestration, and improve the overall performance of mitigation strategies.

One of the fundamental principles of closed-loop nature systems is the replication of ecological processes that cycle carbon and other nutrients through vegetation, soils, and water bodies. These systems are inherently regenerative, relying on feedback loops that maintain system stability and productivity. By designing infrastructure and land-use practices that support these natural cycles, it is possible to embed carbon mitigation within everyday activities, reducing reliance on externally driven technological interventions.

For example, agroecological systems that incorporate composting, cover cropping, and agroforestry practices can retain carbon within soils and biomass while supporting food production. These practices close the loop between organic waste and soil fertility, preventing emissions from decomposition and enhancing long-term carbon storage. Similarly, urban green infrastructure—such as bioswales, green roofs, and urban forests—captures atmospheric carbon while managing stormwater and improving air quality. These elements function as part of a local ecological cycle, with organic material, moisture, and nutrients continually circulating through the system.

Circular water management is another key aspect of closed-loop mitigation. Systems that capture, treat, and reuse water—such as rainwater harvesting, greywater recycling, and constructed wetlands—reduce the need for energy-intensive water extraction and treatment. In turn, this reduces indirect carbon emissions. At the same time, vegetated water systems store carbon in plant biomass and soils, contributing directly to sequestration goals.

Waste systems designed for circularity also support closed-loop carbon mitigation. Organic waste can be processed through composting or anaerobic digestion to produce soil amendments and renewable energy. When returned to natural or agricultural systems, compost enriches soils and promotes biological activity that supports further carbon uptake. Anaerobic digestion provides biogas as an alternative to fossil fuels, helping offset carbon emissions from conventional energy sources.

Maximizing the mitigation potential of closed-loop systems requires coordinated planning, design, and governance. Systems must be tailored to local ecological conditions and supported by monitoring and adaptive management to ensure their continued performance. Materials used in system construction and maintenance should be chosen based on lifecycle carbon impacts, and management practices should prioritize long-term function over short-term efficiency gains.

Ultimately, closed-loop nature systems offer a pathway to more integrated, decentralized, and adaptive approaches to carbon mitigation. By aligning human systems with ecological processes, these models enhance resilience and provide long-term mitigation benefits while supporting biodiversity, water regulation, and social well-being. As such, they represent a valuable component of comprehensive climate strategies grounded in nature and circular design.

Chapter 5: Climate Adaptation: Resilience through Circular NBS

This chapter focuses on how circular NBS contribute to climate adaptation by enhancing the resilience of both human and ecological systems. As climate impacts intensify—including extreme heat, flooding, and ecosystem disruption—there is a growing need for adaptive strategies that work with natural processes and support long-term system flexibility.

Circular NBS offer integrated responses by managing resources efficiently while restoring natural functions that buffer climate risks. These solutions not only reduce exposure and sensitivity to climate hazards but also build adaptive capacity through regenerative design, decentralized systems, and feedback-driven management.

The chapter explores the limitations of conventional adaptation tools and presents circular NBS as multifunctional alternatives that strengthen resilience across urban and rural contexts. It highlights the value of designing for adaptation through inclusive, system-based approaches that align environmental performance with community needs.

Defining Climate Resilience Through NBS

Climate resilience refers to the capacity of systems—ecological, social, and built—to anticipate, absorb, adapt to, and recover from climate-related shocks and stresses while maintaining essential functions and structures. In the context of accelerating climate change, enhancing resilience has become a central objective of urban planning, infrastructure development, and environmental management. NBS provide a practical and scalable approach to building resilience by leveraging the adaptive capacities of ecosystems and integrating them into human systems.

NBS support resilience by using natural processes and green infrastructure to reduce vulnerability and enhance adaptive capacity. Unlike traditional grey infrastructure, which is often static and single-purpose, NBS are dynamic and multifunctional. They offer the flexibility to respond to uncertain and evolving climate conditions, delivering benefits across multiple dimensions. For example, restored wetlands can absorb floodwaters, filter pollutants, and provide habitat, while urban forests can reduce heat stress, sequester carbon, and improve air quality.

One of the defining characteristics of NBS in building climate resilience is their ability to provide ecosystem services that buffer environmental extremes. Vegetated areas help moderate temperature fluctuations, reduce the urban heat island effect, and enhance local cooling through evapotranspiration. Similarly, natural and semi-natural water systems help regulate hydrological cycles by increasing infiltration, reducing runoff, and maintaining groundwater recharge. These functions reduce exposure to hazards such as floods, droughts, and heatwaves.

NBS also contribute to resilience by strengthening social and ecological systems. Green spaces improve public health, promote social cohesion, and offer recreational and educational opportunities. Involving communities in the planning, implementation, and maintenance of NBS fosters local ownership and enhances social capital, which are essential components of resilience. On the ecological side, biodiversity-rich systems are more stable and capable of adapting to change, supporting long-term ecological integrity and functionality.

Another important aspect of NBS is their capacity for co-benefits. While enhancing climate resilience, NBS also address other sustainability goals such as biodiversity conservation, water quality improvement, and carbon sequestration. This integrated performance makes them particularly attractive in contexts where multiple environmental and development objectives must be pursued simultaneously. In resource-constrained settings, multifunctionality adds value by maximizing the return on investment and reducing the need for parallel interventions.

Resilience through NBS also includes the principle of adaptive management. As ecosystems and climate conditions evolve, NBS can be monitored and adjusted to maintain performance and relevance. This flexibility contrasts with conventional approaches that often require significant redesign or replacement in response to changing conditions. NBS can be expanded, replicated, or modified based on ongoing feedback, enhancing their long-term contribution to climate resilience.

In summary, NBS define and support climate resilience by enhancing the capacity of systems to withstand, recover from, and adapt to climate-related challenges. Through ecosystem-based functions, community engagement, and multifunctional design, NBS represent a proactive, cost-effective, and sustainable approach to building resilience across scales and sectors.

Limitations of Conventional Adaptation Tools

Conventional climate adaptation tools, often grounded in engineered or technological solutions, have played a significant role in reducing vulnerability to climate-related hazards. These include flood levees, seawalls, dams, drainage systems, air conditioning technologies, and drought-resistant infrastructure. While such tools can provide immediate or localized relief from climate stressors, they present several limitations when considered from long-term, systems-based, and sustainability-oriented perspectives. These limitations are increasingly relevant in a context of rising climate uncertainty, growing urban populations, and the need for adaptive, inclusive, and ecologically aligned solutions.

A primary limitation of conventional adaptation tools is their often static and inflexible nature. Many engineered solutions are designed for specific risk thresholds based on historical climate data. As climate change accelerates and extreme weather events become more intense and less predictable, infrastructure built to past standards may quickly become outdated. Inflexible systems can fail under stress conditions they were not designed to withstand, leading to increased risk of infrastructure failure and higher repair or replacement costs.

Another challenge lies in the single-function design of most conventional tools. Traditional flood defenses, for example, may protect against inundation but do not provide additional benefits such as water purification, biodiversity support, or recreational value. This lack of multifunctionality reduces the overall efficiency and resilience of the system. In contrast, nature-based and integrated solutions tend to offer co-benefits that extend across environmental, social, and economic dimensions, maximizing returns on investment.

Environmental externalities also present a significant concern. Many conventional adaptation tools are associated with adverse environmental impacts. For instance, hard coastal defenses can accelerate erosion downstream or disrupt sediment transport, negatively affecting marine and shoreline ecosystems. Similarly, large-scale water diversion or drainage systems can alter hydrological cycles, degrade wetlands, and reduce groundwater recharge. These unintended consequences can reduce the adaptive capacity of natural systems and result in the long-term degradation of ecosystem services.

The high costs of construction, operation, and maintenance further limit the scalability and accessibility of conventional tools, particularly in low-income or resource-constrained settings. Many engineered adaptations require substantial capital investment, specialized technical knowledge, and long-term financial commitments. In some contexts, this can divert resources from other critical sectors, such as healthcare or education, or lead to inequities where only affluent areas receive adequate protection.

Social limitations are also evident. Conventional infrastructure projects are often planned and implemented in a top-down manner with limited community engagement. This can result in a misalignment between adaptation measures and local needs or values. Additionally, such approaches may overlook traditional knowledge, community resilience practices, and socio-cultural dynamics that are essential for effective and inclusive adaptation.

Conventional adaptation measures also tend to reinforce existing development models rather than promote systemic transformation. By focusing on technical fixes, they may obscure the underlying drivers of vulnerability, such as land-use decisions, economic inequality, or poor environmental governance. This can result in maladaptation—where actions taken to reduce risk in one area inadvertently increase vulnerability elsewhere or in the future.

Finally, the siloed implementation of conventional adaptation tools often limits their integration into broader urban planning or environmental management frameworks. Fragmented approaches can hinder coordination across sectors such as water, energy, housing, and transportation, reducing overall system resilience and missing opportunities for synergies and efficiencies.

In conclusion, while conventional adaptation tools provide necessary protection in many contexts, they are insufficient as standalone strategies in the face of complex and dynamic climate challenges. Their limitations in terms of flexibility, environmental impact, cost, and inclusivity highlight the need for complementary or alternative approaches. NBS, when combined with circular design principles, offer pathways for overcoming many of these constraints and supporting more resilient, integrated, and adaptive systems.

Circular NBS for Water, Heat, and Disaster Buffering

Circular NBS integrate the principles of closed-loop resource management with the regenerative capacity of ecosystems to enhance urban and regional resilience to water-related stress, heat extremes, and disaster risks. By designing with nature and aligning interventions with circular flows of energy, water, and materials, circular NBS provide multifunctional responses to climate challenges while restoring ecological function and reducing resource consumption. Their application in water management, thermal regulation, and disaster buffering offers sustainable and scalable alternatives to conventional infrastructure.

Water Management

Water-related risks—including flooding, drought, and water pollution—are being intensified by climate change, urbanization, and unsustainable land-use practices. Conventional water management systems, typically linear in design, collect, treat, and discharge water without reintegrating it into natural or urban systems. In contrast, circular NBS manage water as a regenerative resource, utilizing natural processes and closed-loop systems to retain, treat, and reuse water at various scales.

Rain gardens, bioswales, wetlands, and green roofs are examples of NBS that mimic natural hydrology by slowing and infiltrating stormwater. These systems help reduce peak runoff volumes, prevent flash floods, and replenish groundwater. By filtering water through vegetation and soil, they also remove pollutants, improving water quality before it reenters natural systems. Importantly, these features can be integrated into urban landscapes with limited space, such as along streets, in parking lots, and on rooftops.

Circularity is introduced when stormwater is not simply diverted but retained, stored, and reused. For example, captured rainwater from green roofs can be redirected to irrigate urban gardens or flush toilets, reducing demand on potable water systems. Treated greywater can be used to support urban vegetation or recharge groundwater aquifers, forming a cycle of continuous water use within a defined boundary. These interventions not only reduce stress on municipal infrastructure but also reduce energy requirements for water pumping and treatment, thereby cutting emissions.

Heat Mitigation

Urban heat is a growing concern in many regions, driven by the heat island effect, loss of vegetation, and increasing global temperatures. Circular NBS offer effective strategies for passive cooling and thermal regulation by incorporating vegetation and water features into the built environment. Trees, green walls, and vegetated corridors provide shade, increase evapotranspiration, and reduce the absorption of heat by surfaces. These features lower ambient temperatures, improve thermal comfort, and reduce the need for energy-intensive air conditioning.

Circularity in this context involves the reuse of resources—such as using harvested rainwater to maintain green spaces or selecting locally available, low-carbon materials for green infrastructure components. When implemented across multiple urban zones, these systems create cooling networks that are more effective than isolated interventions. Additionally, organic waste can be composted and used to nourish vegetation, supporting plant health and maximizing cooling benefits over time.

Heat buffering through circular NBS extends beyond vegetation. Constructed wetlands, water plazas, and retention ponds not only manage stormwater but also act as thermal regulators. Open water bodies absorb heat during the day and release it at night, moderating temperature fluctuations. By designing such systems to serve multiple functions—such as recreation, flood management, and cooling—cities can achieve climate adaptation objectives while enhancing urban livability.

Disaster Buffering

Circular NBS also enhance resilience to natural disasters, including floods, landslides, and coastal storms. In many cases, conventional infrastructure such as levees or seawalls provides rigid protection that may fail or degrade under extreme conditions. By contrast, nature-based systems offer flexibility, redundancy, and self-regeneration—key characteristics of resilient infrastructure.

In flood-prone regions, restored floodplains, riparian buffers, and reconnected waterways create space for water to flow and be temporarily stored during peak rainfall events. These systems reduce downstream flood risks while supporting biodiversity and groundwater recharge. By using organic materials, natural gradients, and diverse vegetation, such systems maintain their effectiveness over time and adapt to changing hydrological patterns.

In coastal areas, mangroves, dunes, and salt marshes provide natural defense against storm surges and erosion. These ecosystems dissipate wave energy, trap sediment, and build land elevation, forming a living barrier that grows stronger with time. Circular design principles enhance these functions by ensuring the reuse of biomass and organic material, promoting natural regeneration, and minimizing external inputs. Restoration efforts that use locally sourced materials, such as recycled coir logs or natural geotextiles, further reduce the environmental footprint of implementation.

Slope stabilization using bioengineering—such as vegetative cover, root reinforcement, and organic erosion control structures—provides another example of circular NBS for disaster risk reduction. Unlike concrete or steel-based systems, these approaches integrate naturally into landscapes, require minimal maintenance, and support long-term ecological function. By closing nutrient and material loops and enhancing ecosystem structure, they contribute to both hazard mitigation and landscape regeneration.

Co-Benefits and Integration

The integration of circular principles with NBS enhances the multifunctionality, efficiency, and sustainability of interventions. In addition to water, heat, and disaster buffering, circular NBS generate co-benefits such as biodiversity conservation, urban greening, food production, and community engagement. These benefits strengthen the socio-ecological fabric of cities and regions, supporting well-being and reducing vulnerability across populations.

Furthermore, circular NBS can be modular and scalable, allowing them to be implemented incrementally and adapted over time. This makes them particularly useful in areas with limited budgets or high levels of spatial variability. Combined with digital technologies for monitoring and adaptive management, circular NBS can be optimized for local conditions and adjusted to meet evolving climate risks.

Institutional support, cross-sector collaboration, and capacity-building are essential for mainstreaming circular NBS into policy and practice. This includes updating planning regulations, incorporating NBS into infrastructure investment frameworks, and building technical knowledge among planners, engineers, and communities. When supported by enabling governance structures, circular NBS can transition from isolated projects to systemic approaches embedded in urban and regional development.

In summary, circular NBS offer practical and effective strategies for buffering against water-related hazards, heat stress, and disasters. By closing resource loops and harnessing natural processes, they enhance climate resilience while delivering multiple co-benefits. Their adaptability, multifunctionality, and ecological grounding make them key tools in designing regenerative, resilient cities and landscapes in an era of climate uncertainty.

Adaptive Capacity Through Regenerative Design

Adaptive capacity refers to the ability of systems—ecological, social, and built—to adjust to changing conditions, absorb disturbances, and reorganize while maintaining their core functions and structure. In the context of a changing climate, developing adaptive capacity is essential to manage increasing uncertainty and complexity. Regenerative design, which focuses on enhancing the health and vitality of systems through integration with natural processes, provides a practical and forward-looking framework for building this capacity across scales.

Regenerative design differs from conventional sustainability approaches by going beyond minimizing negative impacts to actively restoring, renewing, and evolving systems. This approach prioritizes resilience, multifunctionality, and self-sufficiency, making it well-suited for addressing the dynamic nature of climate risks. Through regenerative design, built environments, landscapes, and infrastructure are conceived not as static assets but as evolving components of socio-ecological systems.

A central principle of regenerative design is the alignment of human-made systems with the cycles and functions of natural systems. This includes designing buildings, infrastructure, and landscapes that work with local climate, hydrology, and ecology. For example, buildings can be oriented to maximize natural ventilation and solar gain, while green infrastructure can be positioned to intercept stormwater and enhance biodiversity. These interventions increase the system's ability to respond to environmental stressors, improving both short-term responsiveness and long-term adaptability.

Regenerative design also emphasizes diversity and redundancy—two features associated with ecological resilience. Incorporating a variety of elements that serve similar functions, such as different types of vegetation in a green space or multiple pathways for water retention, ensures that if one component fails, others can continue to operate. This approach contrasts with highly centralized or single-function systems that are more vulnerable to disruption.

Modularity and scalability further support adaptive capacity. Regenerative systems are often designed as modular units that can be expanded, adapted, or reconfigured as conditions change. This allows for phased implementation, incremental investment, and localized responses to emerging needs. For instance, a green corridor designed with regenerative principles can be extended over time to

56

connect additional habitats or neighborhoods, strengthening ecological and social connectivity.

Community involvement is another key aspect of regenerative design that contributes to adaptive capacity. Engaging local stakeholders in co-design, stewardship, and monitoring fosters a sense of ownership and builds the social capital necessary for ongoing adaptation. Communities that are actively involved in shaping their environment are more likely to identify emerging challenges and respond in a timely and coordinated manner.

Regenerative systems are also inherently learning systems. Through ongoing monitoring, feedback, and iteration, these systems evolve in response to performance and contextual shifts. Adaptive management—where decisions are regularly reviewed and adjusted based on outcomes—ensures that regenerative interventions remain effective under changing conditions.

In summary, regenerative design enhances adaptive capacity by embedding flexibility, resilience, and responsiveness into the fabric of human and ecological systems. By designing for continuous renewal and alignment with natural processes, regenerative approaches offer a pathway for navigating uncertainty and supporting long-term climate resilience.

Chapter 6: Circular Economy Principles in Ecosystem Service Design

This chapter examines how circular economy principles can be applied to enhance and sustain ecosystem services—the essential benefits that nature provides to people. These include provisioning services like food and water, regulating services such as climate and flood control, and supporting services that maintain biodiversity and soil health.

Linear systems often disrupt or deplete these services through extraction, pollution, and waste. In contrast, circular approaches aim to preserve ecological function by designing systems that minimize resource loss, regenerate natural capital, and maintain continuous flows of ecosystem benefits.

The chapter outlines the pressures placed on ecosystem services by traditional development models and explores how circular design can restore and strengthen these functions. It emphasizes the importance of systems thinking, multifunctionality, and long-term stewardship in aligning ecological health with sustainable development objectives.

Overview of Ecosystem Services

Ecosystem services are the benefits that humans derive from nature. They represent the direct and indirect contributions of ecosystems to human well-being and are fundamental to sustaining environmental health, economic development, and social stability. Categorizing and understanding these services enables policymakers, planners, and resource managers to recognize the value of ecosystems in decision-making and design interventions that align with long-term sustainability goals.

Ecosystem services are commonly classified into four categories: provisioning, regulating, cultural, and supporting services.

Provisioning services include tangible products obtained from ecosystems such as food, fresh water, timber, fiber, and medicinal resources. These services are essential for livelihoods and economic activity, particularly in agriculture, forestry, and fisheries.

Regulating services are the benefits obtained from the regulation of ecosystem processes. These include climate regulation through carbon sequestration, water purification, flood control, air quality maintenance, and disease regulation. These services play a crucial role in moderating environmental conditions and protecting communities from natural hazards and pollution.

Cultural services refer to the non-material benefits people obtain from ecosystems. These include recreational experiences, aesthetic enjoyment, spiritual fulfillment, educational opportunities, and cultural identity. Green and blue spaces in urban areas, for example, contribute significantly to mental and physical well-being, community cohesion, and the livability of cities.

Supporting services underpin all other ecosystem services by maintaining the fundamental ecological processes necessary for life. These include nutrient cycling, soil formation, primary production, and habitat provision. Although not always directly visible or measurable in economic terms, supporting services are critical to the stability and functioning of ecosystems over time.

The interconnectedness of these services highlights the multifunctionality of ecosystems. For instance, a healthy wetland simultaneously stores carbon (climate regulation), filters pollutants (water purification), provides habitat for species (supporting services), and supports recreational activities (cultural services). Recognizing this multifunctionality is essential for designing integrated management approaches that deliver multiple benefits simultaneously.

Urbanization, land-use change, pollution, and climate change are placing growing pressure on ecosystems and diminishing their capacity to deliver services. This loss of ecosystem functionality can lead to increased vulnerability, reduced resilience, and higher economic and social costs. As a result, there is a growing interest in NBS and circular design strategies that restore or enhance ecosystem service provision while meeting development needs.

Quantifying and valuing ecosystem services has become a key area of focus in environmental planning and economics. While some services have market values, many are non-market and require alternative valuation methods. Incorporating ecosystem service assessments into policy, planning, and infrastructure design helps ensure that the benefits of ecosystems are fully considered in decision-making processes.

In summary, ecosystem services provide the foundation for human well-being and ecological resilience. Understanding their categories, functions, and interdependencies is essential for managing natural capital effectively. Integrating ecosystem service thinking into spatial planning, development, and governance frameworks supports the creation of sustainable, regenerative systems aligned with environmental limits and societal needs.

Linear Pressures on Provisioning and Regulating Services

Linear economic and development models exert significant pressure on ecosystem services, particularly provisioning and regulating services. These pressures arise from the extraction–consumption–disposal pathway that characterizes most industrial systems and infrastructure planning. In such models, natural resources are treated as inputs to be used and discarded, with limited consideration for regeneration or the maintenance of ecological function. Over time, this approach leads to the degradation of ecosystems and diminishes their ability to provide essential services.

Provisioning services—including food, water, timber, and raw materials—are among the most directly affected by linear pressures.

Unsustainable agricultural practices, deforestation, overfishing, and water abstraction often prioritize short-term yield over long-term ecological health. For instance, intensive monoculture farming can deplete soil nutrients, increase vulnerability to pests and diseases, and reduce biodiversity. Similarly, overextraction of groundwater for irrigation and urban supply can lower water tables and lead to the collapse of dependent ecosystems such as wetlands and riparian habitats.

Linear extraction methods often disregard the carrying capacity of ecosystems, leading to resource depletion and ecosystem stress. Logging without reforestation, for example, undermines both the provisioning and regulating capacities of forest ecosystems. Not only is timber supply disrupted over the long term, but the loss of forest cover also affects regulating services such as climate regulation, water filtration, and erosion control. The result is a feedback loop where ecosystem degradation undermines the services that human systems rely on.

Regulating services are particularly vulnerable to the cumulative impacts of pollution, land-use change, and climate variability—often driven or exacerbated by linear systems. For example, traditional stormwater infrastructure that channels runoff into rivers or oceans removes water from the landscape without treatment or infiltration. This disrupts natural hydrological cycles, reduces groundwater recharge, and often results in degraded water quality due to the accumulation of pollutants. In contrast, ecosystems such as wetlands and vegetated swales regulate water flows while filtering contaminants—functions that are diminished when land is paved or engineered in ways that bypass natural processes.

Air quality regulation is another example of a regulating service under pressure from linear systems. Fossil fuel combustion in transport and industry releases pollutants that vegetation and soil organisms would normally help absorb or break down. Urban expansion that replaces green areas with impermeable surfaces further limits the ecosystem's capacity to regulate air quality, contributing to public health issues and reducing overall environmental quality.

Climate regulation through carbon storage is similarly affected. The removal of vegetative cover and soil disturbance from land-use conversion releases stored carbon, while degraded ecosystems lose the ability to sequester carbon effectively. This not only increases greenhouse gas concentrations but also diminishes the landscape's buffering capacity against climate impacts such as temperature extremes and storm events.

Moreover, linear approaches often treat ecosystem services as isolated functions, leading to fragmented responses that fail to address the underlying ecological dynamics. The disconnection between provisioning and regulating services results in management strategies that may secure one benefit at the expense of another. For instance, water-intensive agriculture may ensure food production in the short term but degrade aquatic ecosystems and reduce long-term water availability and quality.

To address these pressures, there is a growing need to transition from linear to circular and regenerative systems that maintain and enhance the functionality of provisioning and regulating services. This includes integrating NBS into land-use and infrastructure planning, adopting sustainable resource management practices, and recognizing the interdependencies between different types of ecosystem services.

In summary, linear development and resource use models place significant strain on provisioning and regulating services by prioritizing extraction over regeneration and disconnection over integration. Responding to these pressures requires systemic change in how natural resources are valued, managed, and replenished, ensuring ecosystems remain capable of supporting both human needs and ecological stability over the long term.

Circular Design for Restoring Service Flows

Circular design offers a structured and systems-based approach to restoring and sustaining ecosystem service flows, particularly those that have been disrupted or diminished by linear development practices. By emulating natural cycles and prioritizing resource efficiency, regeneration, and integration, circular design enhances the capacity of ecosystems to deliver provisioning and regulating services over the long term. The application of circular principles in land use, infrastructure, and resource management can re-establish disrupted ecological processes and reorient human activities within environmental limits.

At its core, circular design focuses on retaining the value of resources within systems for as long as possible. In ecosystem service terms, this means designing interventions that sustain or enhance the ecological functions underpinning services such as clean water, fertile soils, healthy air, and stable climate regulation. Unlike conventional systems that often isolate services into discrete management functions, circular approaches aim to optimize flows across systems in a way that maintains multifunctionality and ecological integrity.

Water systems are a prime example of where circular design can be applied to restore regulating and provisioning services. Traditional linear systems extract water from a source, use it once, and then discharge it—often untreated—into receiving bodies. In contrast, circular design promotes decentralized, closed-loop systems that capture, treat, and reuse water within the same landscape. Rainwater harvesting, greywater recycling, and constructed wetlands enable water to cycle through local systems, supporting both human and ecological needs while reducing demand on centralized infrastructure.

These designs also restore key hydrological functions such as infiltration and evapotranspiration, which regulate water quality, quantity, and flow timing. By incorporating vegetation and permeable surfaces into the built environment, circular water management strategies reduce runoff, recharge aquifers, and buffer against floods and droughts. These functions collectively restore the regulating services that are critical to urban and rural water resilience.

Soil and nutrient management is another domain where circular design plays a key role in restoring service flows. Conventional agriculture often relies on external inputs and practices that degrade soil health, reduce biodiversity, and disrupt nutrient cycling. Circular approaches—such as composting, organic farming, agroecology, and regenerative agriculture—close the loop by returning organic matter and nutrients back to the soil. These practices not only reduce the need for synthetic fertilizers but also restore soil structure, increase water retention, and enhance carbon sequestration.

When circular principles are embedded in food systems, organic waste becomes a resource rather than a liability. For instance, food scraps can be processed into compost or biofertilizers that replenish soil health and support productive ecosystems. This reinforces provisioning services such as food production while simultaneously improving regulating services like erosion control, water filtration, and carbon storage.

Urban environments offer further opportunities for restoring service flows through circular design. Green roofs, bioswales, tree-lined streets, and urban agriculture are all elements of regenerative urbanism that contribute to temperature regulation, air purification, and biodiversity support. These features can be planned and managed as part of circular systems that cycle water, nutrients, and materials within neighborhoods or districts.

For example, an integrated urban block might collect and reuse rainwater, compost organic waste on-site, and support vegetation that provides habitat and cooling. Materials used in construction and landscaping could be sourced locally, reused from demolition, or selected for their biodegradability or recyclability. In this way, circular urban design reduces environmental footprints while restoring disrupted flows of ecosystem services.

Material circularity also contributes to restoring service flows by reducing demand on ecosystems for raw inputs and by limiting emissions and pollution associated with extraction and disposal. By designing buildings and products for durability, disassembly, and reuse, pressure is alleviated on ecosystems that supply timber, minerals, and other resources. At the same time, diverting waste from landfills reduces leachate, methane emissions, and other negative externalities that can compromise regulating services like water and air quality.

This extends to infrastructure as well. Circular principles in infrastructure design promote modularity and adaptability, allowing components to be replaced or upgraded without wholesale demolition. Infrastructure can also be designed to integrate nature-based features, such as permeable pavements that support groundwater recharge or transit corridors that double as green corridors for species movement. These multifunctional systems enable human services and ecological services to coexist, reinforcing the feedback loops essential to ecosystem stability.

Energy systems designed with circularity in mind can restore service flows by reducing pollution and supporting local regenerative functions. Distributed renewable energy systems—such as solar panels integrated into buildings—minimize dependence on fossil fuels and associated emissions that degrade air quality and contribute to climate instability. Waste-to-energy systems that process organic materials can generate biogas while producing digestate for soil improvement, completing a circular loop that benefits both energy and ecosystem function.

Governance and planning frameworks are vital to enabling circular design in support of ecosystem service restoration. Zoning regulations, procurement policies, building codes, and infrastructure standards can be revised to encourage integrated, circular approaches. For instance, requiring stormwater to be managed on-site through nature-based methods or mandating the reuse of construction materials can institutionalize circular practices that reinforce ecosystem service flows.

Stakeholder engagement also plays a critical role. Circular systems often rely on decentralized actions—such as household composting, community gardening, or cooperative water reuse—that require behavioral shifts and local coordination. Engaging communities in co-design and stewardship builds the social foundations necessary for maintaining and scaling circular systems over time.

Monitoring and adaptive management ensure that circular systems continue to support ecosystem service restoration as conditions change. Metrics that track soil health, water quality, biodiversity, and resource flows allow for iterative improvements and responsive governance. Digital technologies, such as sensors, GIS, and modeling tools, can support this process by providing real-time data and facilitating scenario planning.

In conclusion, circular design offers a comprehensive and integrated approach to restoring ecosystem service flows. By closing resource loops and aligning built environments with ecological processes, circular strategies regenerate natural capital while supporting essential provisioning and regulating services. When applied across sectors and scales, circular design not only addresses the environmental impacts of linear systems and builds a foundation for resilient and regenerative communities and landscapes.

Systems Thinking for Multifunctional Ecosystem Benefits

Systems thinking is an approach that emphasizes the interconnections and interdependencies among components within a system. Applied to environmental management and design, it encourages a holistic view of ecosystems, recognizing that changes in one part of a system can influence multiple others. In the context of NBS and circular design, systems thinking is essential for realizing multifunctional ecosystem benefits—those that simultaneously address environmental, social, and economic objectives through integrated, synergistic interventions.

Multifunctionality refers to the ability of a single intervention or system to deliver multiple benefits across different domains. For example, an urban green corridor may provide flood mitigation (regulating service), recreational space (cultural service), wildlife habitat (supporting service), and enhanced air quality (regulating service). By identifying and designing for these overlapping benefits, planners and practitioners can maximize the efficiency and effectiveness of nature-based and circular strategies.

Systems thinking supports multifunctionality by shifting the focus from single-purpose infrastructure or land uses to integrated, landscape-scale solutions. This involves considering how different ecosystem services interact and how interventions can be configured to enhance, rather than compete with, one another. For instance, integrating urban agriculture with stormwater management infrastructure can produce food, manage water runoff, and improve soil health, all within the same footprint.

The approach also accounts for feedback loops and non-linear relationships. In ecosystems, benefits are not always proportional to inputs; small changes can lead to significant impacts, both positive and negative. Systems thinking helps decision-makers understand the thresholds, trade-offs, and co-benefits associated with interventions. For example, restoring a wetland may improve water quality and carbon storage, but it may also require land-use trade-offs or changes in drainage patterns. By analyzing these dynamics in advance, projects can be designed to optimize outcomes and avoid unintended consequences.

Cross-scale interactions are another important consideration. Ecosystem services are often influenced by processes occurring at multiple spatial and temporal scales. For example, a reforestation effort in a watershed may have long-term benefits for downstream flood regulation and sediment control. Systems thinking encourages coordination across sectors and jurisdictions to ensure that interventions at one scale support, rather than undermine, outcomes at another.

Additionally, systems thinking reinforces the need for adaptive management. Ecosystems and human systems are dynamic, and interventions must be flexible enough to respond to new information, changing conditions, or unexpected outcomes. Monitoring, evaluation, and iterative learning are therefore integral components of a systems-based approach.

Stakeholder engagement is also central to systems thinking. Understanding how different communities value and interact with ecosystem services can inform more equitable and context-sensitive designs. Co-benefits are more likely to be achieved when diverse perspectives are integrated into planning processes and when responsibilities for maintenance and governance are shared.

In summary, systems thinking provides a foundation for designing and managing interventions that deliver multifunctional ecosystem benefits. By considering the complexity and interconnectedness of ecological and human systems, it supports the creation of integrated, resilient, and adaptive solutions aligned with long-term sustainability goals.

Chapter 7: Governance and Policy for Integrating NBS and Circular Design

This chapter explores the governance and policy frameworks needed to support the integration of NBS and circular design principles. Effective implementation of these approaches requires coordinated action across sectors, levels of government, and stakeholder groups, supported by enabling regulations, institutions, and planning processes.

Fragmented governance and siloed decision-making often hinder the delivery of integrated environmental solutions. Addressing these barriers involves developing cross-sector models, aligning policies, and institutionalizing regenerative practices within existing administrative systems.

The chapter examines the political, institutional, and financial drivers that influence uptake, and outlines pathways for scaling circular NBS through collaborative governance, inclusive planning, and supportive legal and regulatory instruments. It highlights the importance of systemic coordination to ensure durable, equitable, and scalable outcomes.

Fragmented Governance and Siloed Planning

Fragmented governance and siloed planning are persistent challenges that hinder the effective implementation of integrated environmental strategies, including those based on NBS and circular design principles. These challenges arise when institutional responsibilities, policy frameworks, and planning processes are divided across sectors, jurisdictions, or administrative levels without sufficient coordination. As a result, efforts to manage land, water, energy, biodiversity, and infrastructure are often undertaken in isolation, reducing opportunities for synergy and increasing the risk of inefficiencies, duplication, or unintended trade-offs.

In many governance systems, responsibilities for environmental management are divided among different agencies or departments—such as those for water, waste, transport, housing, and agriculture—each with distinct mandates, funding streams, and regulatory instruments. This sectoral structure may be reinforced by legal and institutional frameworks that define roles narrowly, leaving limited scope for collaboration or integrated decision-making. For instance, a department responsible for urban drainage may not be mandated to consider ecological restoration, while an agency focused on biodiversity may have little influence over urban development policies.

Siloed planning extends beyond government structures to include spatial planning, investment processes, and infrastructure design. Land-use plans, capital investment strategies, and building codes are often developed independently, without reference to broader environmental systems or cross-sectoral objectives. This separation limits the potential for co-locating functions, sharing resources, or achieving multifunctional outcomes. For example, transport corridors may be designed without consideration for green infrastructure connectivity, or housing developments may proceed without integrating circular water or waste systems.

The consequences of fragmentation include suboptimal use of public resources, missed opportunities for innovation, and diminished resilience to environmental stress. When strategies are not aligned, interventions may inadvertently undermine one another. A classic example is the construction of hard flood defenses that protect specific areas while increasing flood risk downstream. Similarly, linear infrastructure may fragment ecosystems that could otherwise support nature-based stormwater management, biodiversity corridors, or carbon sinks.

Fragmentation also affects monitoring, evaluation, and data sharing. Without harmonized systems for collecting and analyzing data across sectors, it is difficult to assess the cumulative impacts of policies or to adapt strategies in response to changing conditions.

Inconsistent data standards and a lack of interoperability between information systems further complicate coordination efforts.

From a policy perspective, fragmented governance can lead to conflicting objectives, regulatory gaps, or inconsistent enforcement. In some cases, this creates uncertainty for stakeholders or discourages investment in integrated solutions. It can also hinder the mainstreaming of circular and nature-based approaches, which often require collaborative governance, shared responsibilities, and flexible funding mechanisms.

Addressing fragmentation requires institutional reform, policy alignment, and deliberate efforts to foster interdepartmental and cross-sectoral collaboration. This includes the creation of integrated planning frameworks, interagency task forces, and shared governance platforms that encourage joint problem-solving. Mechanisms for participatory planning and stakeholder engagement can also help bridge silos by aligning strategies with local knowledge and priorities.

In summary, fragmented governance and siloed planning are structural barriers to the implementation of holistic and regenerative approaches. Overcoming these barriers is essential for enabling coordinated action, maximizing co-benefits, and supporting long-term sustainability and resilience goals.

Political and Institutional Drivers of Change

Political and institutional drivers play a central role in shaping the conditions under which circular design principles and NBS can be adopted and scaled. These drivers include leadership, policy direction, regulatory frameworks, institutional mandates, financing structures, and administrative capacity. Together, they influence how priorities are set, resources are allocated, and implementation processes unfold across sectors and governance levels.

Political leadership is often a catalyst for advancing integrated and forward-looking environmental strategies. When elected officials or senior government leaders champion sustainability agendas, they can mobilize public support, direct funding, and align institutional goals with long-term climate and biodiversity targets. Political will is particularly important in overcoming inertia within established systems and in legitimizing innovative approaches that may challenge conventional planning or investment models.

Policy coherence is another critical driver. Effective change requires alignment between national development strategies, sectoral policies, and local implementation frameworks. For example, climate adaptation policies that explicitly reference NBS and circular economy principles provide a foundation for their inclusion in infrastructure projects, land-use planning, and public procurement. Likewise, integration across environmental, social, and economic policy domains creates the conditions for systemic approaches that deliver multiple co-benefits.

Institutional mandates and structures also shape the ability to implement integrated solutions. Organizations that are mandated to work across sectors, or that are explicitly tasked with sustainability and resilience, are more likely to support cross-cutting initiatives. Conversely, narrowly defined mandates may constrain institutions from engaging in collaborative or experimental work. Institutional flexibility—both in terms of organizational design and procedural rules—can enable adaptive management and interagency coordination, key elements for implementing NBS and circular systems effectively.

Administrative capacity is a practical determinant of institutional performance. This includes the availability of skilled personnel, access to data and decision-support tools, and the ability to manage complex, multi-stakeholder processes. Capacity-building initiatives that enhance understanding of circular and nature-based approaches across government agencies can significantly influence uptake and implementation quality. Partnerships with academic institutions,

72

civil society, and the private sector can supplement internal capacity and introduce new expertise and perspectives.

Legal and regulatory frameworks establish the formal rules within which decisions are made and resources are managed. Enabling regulations—such as those that permit the use of alternative materials, incentivize decentralized infrastructure, or recognize ecosystem services in planning—can accelerate the shift toward circular and nature-based models. Conversely, restrictive or outdated regulations can limit innovation, deter investment, or maintain reliance on grey infrastructure and linear resource use.

Public finance mechanisms also act as institutional drivers. Budget allocations, fiscal incentives, and investment programs can direct funding toward preferred outcomes. For example, green bonds, performance-based grants, or climate funds can prioritize projects that deliver ecosystem co-benefits, support resource efficiency, or contribute to emissions reduction. Importantly, the criteria used in financing decisions shape the types of projects that are viable and the extent to which integrated solutions are prioritized.

Transparency, accountability, and participatory governance are additional institutional features that support change. Decision-making processes that engage diverse stakeholders—including communities, private sector actors, and knowledge institutions—tend to generate more context-appropriate, accepted, and enduring outcomes. Inclusion and dialogue also help identify synergies and address trade-offs across objectives and sectors.

In summary, political and institutional drivers of change are foundational to the success of circular and nature-based approaches. Leadership, policy coherence, regulatory reform, institutional mandates, and capacity all influence how effectively these strategies are adopted, integrated, and sustained. Strengthening these drivers through deliberate design and governance reform is essential for enabling the transition toward more resilient, regenerative systems.

Coordinated Policy and Cross-Sector Governance Models

Effective implementation of circular design principles and NBS depends on coordinated policy frameworks and cross-sector governance models. These models are necessary to overcome institutional fragmentation, align objectives across different levels of government, and promote integrated approaches that reflect the interconnected nature of environmental, social, and economic systems. By enabling collaboration across traditionally siloed domains, coordinated governance supports multifunctional outcomes, enhances resource efficiency, and improves the long-term resilience of human and ecological systems.

The Need for Coordination

Policy and planning processes have traditionally been structured around single-sector mandates, such as transport, housing, water, or energy. While this specialization supports technical expertise and accountability, it often limits opportunities to address complex, interrelated challenges such as climate change, biodiversity loss, and resource degradation. Fragmented approaches can result in inefficiencies, duplicated efforts, and even counterproductive outcomes—for example, infrastructure development that undermines ecosystem restoration or land-use policies that conflict with climate adaptation goals.

Coordinated policy frameworks respond to these limitations by establishing shared goals, harmonizing planning instruments, and aligning implementation mechanisms across sectors. They create a foundation for collaboration, enabling decision-makers to consider co-benefits, manage trade-offs, and design interventions that are coherent at multiple scales.

Integrated Planning and Policy Alignment

One key element of coordinated governance is integrated planning. This involves the development of policies and plans that are cross-sectoral in scope and spatially aligned. For instance, a regional development strategy might incorporate objectives related to land use, water management, transport, housing, and biodiversity in a single framework. This integration allows for strategic prioritization, where investments and interventions are selected based on their ability to deliver multiple outcomes.

Policy alignment across levels of government is equally important. National frameworks should provide clear direction and enabling conditions for subnational implementation, while allowing for local adaptation and innovation. For example, national climate policies can mandate or incentivize the use of NBS and circular approaches, while municipalities develop local plans and regulations that operationalize these strategies on the ground. Coherence between national and local efforts ensures consistency, reduces gaps in implementation, and facilitates access to financing and technical support.

Cross-Sector Governance Structures

To operationalize coordinated policies, institutional mechanisms are needed to facilitate cross-sector governance. These may include inter-ministerial committees, cross-departmental task forces, or multi-agency platforms that bring together stakeholders from different policy domains. These bodies support joint planning, information sharing, and collective problem-solving. Their effectiveness often depends on clear mandates, adequate resources, and mechanisms for accountability.

At the municipal level, cross-sector coordination can be embedded in planning departments, sustainability units, or special-purpose entities. For instance, a city may establish a green infrastructure office responsible for coordinating inputs from water, transport, and parks departments to design integrated solutions. Such units can also serve as hubs for stakeholder engagement, ensuring that diverse perspectives are considered and local knowledge is integrated.

Collaborative Governance and Stakeholder Engagement

Cross-sector governance extends beyond public institutions to include civil society, the private sector, academic institutions, and community organizations. Collaborative governance models create space for these actors to contribute to planning, decision-making, implementation, and monitoring. This inclusivity strengthens legitimacy, increases local ownership, and enhances the quality and durability of outcomes.

Public–private partnerships can play a key role in advancing circular and nature-based strategies, particularly in infrastructure development, innovation, and service delivery. Businesses may invest in green infrastructure, circular product systems, or ecosystem restoration as part of sustainability commitments or regulatory requirements. Engaging the private sector early in the policy and design process helps align incentives and ensure feasibility.

Community-based governance models, such as watershed councils or neighborhood greening initiatives, are effective in addressing place-specific challenges and mobilizing local action. These models often operate at smaller scales, but they contribute to broader governance systems by piloting innovative approaches, monitoring local conditions, and fostering environmental stewardship.

Policy Instruments for Coordination

A variety of policy instruments can support coordinated governance. Strategic frameworks, such as national biodiversity strategies or circular economy roadmaps, establish long-term visions and action plans that span multiple sectors. These frameworks are most effective when supported by implementation tools, including legal mandates, performance targets, funding mechanisms, and technical guidelines.

Regulatory instruments such as integrated environmental planning laws or mandatory impact assessments can require coordination among agencies and sectors. Planning tools like land-use zoning, development permits, and environmental impact assessments can be structured to account for ecosystem services, circular resource flows, and climate risks. By requiring consultation and joint review processes, these tools promote collaboration in design and approval stages.

Incentive mechanisms, including grants, tax benefits, and performance-based financing, can encourage cross-sectoral collaboration and innovation. Funding programs that require joint proposals from multiple departments or organizations can help break down silos and promote shared responsibility. Similarly, reporting requirements that assess co-benefits—such as emissions reductions, biodiversity gains, and community engagement—can reinforce integrated approaches.

Data Integration and Shared Information Systems

Reliable data and knowledge are essential for coordinated governance. Integrated information systems that bring together data on land use, climate risks, water flows, biodiversity, and infrastructure enable stakeholders to assess conditions holistically and make informed decisions. GIS, digital dashboards, and open-data platforms can support spatial analysis, scenario modeling, and performance monitoring.

Cross-sector data sharing is often constrained by incompatible systems, lack of standards, or institutional reluctance. Addressing these barriers requires common data protocols, legal agreements, and investments in digital infrastructure. Data sharing agreements and centralized repositories can enable access to consistent, up-to-date information across departments and agencies.

Challenges and Opportunities

While the benefits of coordinated policy and cross-sector governance are clear, practical challenges remain. Institutional inertia, competing mandates, budgetary constraints, and political dynamics can impede collaboration. Building trust, establishing shared goals, and demonstrating the value of integration are key to overcoming resistance. Pilot projects, demonstration sites, and co-designed initiatives can help build momentum and scale up successful models.

In parallel, emerging frameworks such as the Sustainable Development Goals (SDGs), the Paris Agreement, and the Global Biodiversity Framework offer opportunities to align national and subnational strategies with global targets. These frameworks encourage countries to adopt integrated approaches and provide platforms for knowledge exchange, benchmarking, and financial support.

Conclusion

Coordinated policy and cross-sector governance models are essential for scaling circular and NBS. By fostering alignment, integration, and collaboration across sectors and levels of government, these models enable systemic responses to complex environmental challenges. Strengthening these governance arrangements will be critical to achieving resilient, regenerative, and inclusive development pathways.

Institutionalizing Circular NBS Across Scales

Institutionalizing circular NBS involves embedding their principles and practices into governance systems, planning frameworks, and operational procedures across different scales—from local to national and regional levels. This process is essential for moving beyond pilot projects or isolated applications and ensuring that circular NBS become part of mainstream infrastructure development, land-use planning, and climate adaptation and mitigation strategies.

Scaling circular NBS requires coherent frameworks that connect policy ambition with practical implementation. At the local level, municipalities and urban authorities often lead on spatial planning and public infrastructure development, making them critical actors in institutionalizing NBS. Local governments can integrate circular and nature-based approaches into building codes, land-use plans, zoning regulations, and procurement policies. For instance, stormwater management standards can prioritize green infrastructure, while waste collection systems can support composting and organic resource loops.

At the national level, policy guidance, funding mechanisms, and regulatory frameworks play a foundational role. National governments can establish legal mandates and performance targets that support circular resource flows and ecosystem-based planning. They can also coordinate inter-ministerial efforts to align strategies across environment, housing, infrastructure, and finance portfolios. Incorporating circular NBS into national climate plans, biodiversity strategies, or circular economy roadmaps helps ensure consistent direction and long-term commitment.

At the regional scale, coordination becomes important for managing shared resources such as watersheds, forests, or coastal zones. Regional planning bodies can facilitate cross-jurisdictional collaboration, especially where ecological processes extend beyond administrative boundaries. For example, river basin organizations or metropolitan authorities can align infrastructure investments with ecosystem restoration and circular economy objectives. Regional coordination also allows for standardization in technical approaches and data sharing, increasing efficiency and effectiveness.

Institutionalization also depends on multi-level governance—the interaction between local, regional, and national institutions. Ensuring that policies are coherent and mutually reinforcing across scales prevents fragmentation and supports integrated planning. Mechanisms such as intergovernmental working groups, joint planning platforms, or aligned funding programs can bridge gaps and promote consistency.

Capacity building is another key enabler. Public officials, planners, and practitioners need the skills, tools, and knowledge to design and implement circular NBS effectively. Training programs, technical guidelines, and knowledge exchange platforms can support institutional learning and build the competencies required for scale. Partnerships with academic and research institutions can further strengthen evidence-based decision-making and innovation.

Institutionalization also involves establishing monitoring, reporting, and evaluation systems to track performance and support adaptive management. Defining indicators for ecosystem service delivery, circular resource flows, and climate resilience helps measure outcomes and refine strategies over time. Transparency in reporting also enhances accountability and stakeholder engagement.

In summary, institutionalizing circular NBS across scales requires a coordinated, multi-level effort that aligns policy, planning, and practice. By embedding these approaches into institutional structures, regulatory frameworks, and operational systems, governments can create enabling environments for widespread adoption. This transition supports resilient, regenerative development aligned with long-term ecological, social, and economic goals.

Chapter 8: Financing Nature-Based Circular Solutions

This chapter addresses the financial dimensions of implementing NBS and circular economy strategies, focusing on the tools, barriers, and opportunities associated with funding these integrated approaches. While the environmental and social benefits of NBS and circular systems are well recognized, challenges persist in mobilizing adequate and sustained investment.

Traditional financial models often favor conventional infrastructure and short-term returns, leaving NBS and circular projects underfunded or perceived as high risk. At the same time, emerging financial instruments—such as blended finance, green bonds, and ecosystem valuation tools—are helping to bridge funding gaps and build investor confidence.

The chapter examines structural and market-based financing challenges, the role of sustainable finance in accelerating adoption, and the importance of aligning capital flows with long-term environmental and social outcomes. It highlights how financial innovation and supportive policy frameworks can unlock investment and scale regenerative solutions.

Financing Gaps in Nature-Based Systems

Despite growing recognition of their value, nature-based systems often face significant financing gaps that hinder their widespread implementation and long-term maintenance. These gaps stem from structural, institutional, and market-related challenges that make it difficult for public and private actors to allocate adequate resources to NBS, particularly those aligned with circular design and multifunctional outcomes. Addressing these financing gaps is critical to scaling the impact of NBS and integrating them into mainstream infrastructure and development planning.

One of the primary reasons for underinvestment in NBS is the lack of direct revenue streams. Unlike conventional infrastructure—such as toll roads or energy systems—that may generate predictable income, many NBS deliver public goods and ecosystem services that are not easily monetized. Benefits such as flood regulation, biodiversity conservation, and improved air quality are often diffuse, long-term, and shared across communities, making it difficult to capture returns on investment through market-based mechanisms.

A related issue is the limited integration of NBS into financial planning and budgeting frameworks. Public infrastructure budgets are typically allocated based on established asset classes and cost-benefit assessments that prioritize short-term efficiency and technical certainty. As a result, NBS projects may be overlooked or underfunded due to perceived risks, limited standardization, or a lack of familiarity with their performance metrics. In some cases, funding mechanisms are not designed to accommodate hybrid or decentralized solutions, which can further disadvantage NBS.

Additionally, existing investment models often favor grey infrastructure due to its standardized designs, regulatory familiarity, and track record of implementation. Financial institutions and investors may view NBS as novel or unproven, particularly when compared to traditional engineered alternatives. This perception can increase the cost of capital or reduce the willingness of funders to engage, especially in contexts where project evaluation tools are not adapted to the specificities of nature-based interventions.

Maintenance and lifecycle financing also represent a gap. While NBS may have lower operational costs over time, they require ongoing care, monitoring, and adaptive management to remain effective. Securing funding for these long-term needs can be challenging, particularly when financing mechanisms are structured around one-time capital expenditures without provisions for operational support. This can compromise the durability and performance of NBS investments.

Further complicating financing is the fragmentation of funding sources. NBS often deliver co-benefits across multiple sectors—such as water, health, biodiversity, and urban development—but funding streams are typically siloed within specific departments or policy areas. This fragmentation can result in missed opportunities for cost-sharing or joint investment and may discourage integrated project design.

Finally, a lack of standardized valuation methods makes it difficult to fully account for the economic value of ecosystem services and resilience benefits provided by NBS. Without clear evidence of return on investment, particularly in financial terms, NBS may struggle to compete with traditional infrastructure proposals in budget and funding processes.

In summary, financing gaps in nature-based systems are the result of multiple interrelated barriers. Overcoming them requires a shift in how NBS are valued, budgeted, and integrated into financial and planning systems. Innovative funding approaches, improved metrics, and cross-sector collaboration will be essential to close these gaps and unlock the full potential of circular and nature-based approaches.

Market and Investment Barriers

The expansion of NBS and circular design strategies is increasingly recognized as essential for addressing environmental and climate challenges. However, several market and investment barriers continue to impede the flow of capital into these types of projects. These barriers are rooted in the structure of financial markets, perceptions of risk, a lack of enabling frameworks, and limitations in how value is assessed and captured. Understanding these constraints is important for developing strategies that improve the bankability and scalability of nature-based and circular interventions.

A major barrier is the limited alignment between financial markets and the characteristics of NBS. Financial institutions are accustomed to investing in conventional infrastructure and asset classes that offer clearly defined cash flows, short-to-medium-term returns, and measurable performance metrics. In contrast, NBS often provide non-market benefits such as improved ecosystem health, climate regulation, or social cohesion—values that are difficult to translate into direct financial returns. This disconnect creates uncertainty for investors and can lead to the perception that NBS are high-risk or low-return investments.

Risk perception and lack of track record further deter market participation. Many investors are unfamiliar with the design, operation, and long-term performance of NBS, particularly when compared to more established grey infrastructure. The relatively limited number of large-scale, commercially financed NBS projects contributes to this uncertainty. As a result, investors may be reluctant to allocate capital without guarantees, co-financing, or strong policy backing. This is especially true in contexts where project outcomes depend on environmental variables that can be difficult to control or predict.

Valuation challenges also limit investment. Traditional financial appraisal tools often fail to capture the full value of ecosystem services or the avoided costs associated with nature-based approaches. For example, the cost savings from reduced flood damage, improved health outcomes, or increased biodiversity may not be reflected in investment models. Without standardized methods for incorporating these externalities, NBS projects may appear less competitive when assessed alongside conventional alternatives.

The lack of enabling policy and regulatory frameworks can also present a barrier. In many jurisdictions, existing planning regulations, building codes, and procurement rules are not designed to support circular and nature-based approaches. This can increase the administrative burden on project developers or limit the eligibility of NBS for public funding and investment incentives. In addition, unclear or inconsistent definitions and classifications of NBS and circular infrastructure can make it difficult to integrate them into investment pipelines or reporting frameworks.

Limited access to finance for small-scale or community-based projects further restricts investment. Many NBS initiatives are locally led and tailored to specific environmental or social contexts, resulting in relatively small ticket sizes that do not align with institutional investors' preferences. High transaction costs, low economies of scale, and the absence of aggregated financing mechanisms often make these projects less attractive despite their high local relevance and impact potential.

Finally, a lack of data, performance benchmarks, and standardization inhibits the creation of financial products tailored to NBS. Investors typically rely on consistent data to assess risk, measure returns, and meet reporting requirements. Without a robust evidence base or widely accepted metrics for NBS performance, it is challenging to build confidence among investors or integrate these projects into sustainability-linked investment portfolios.

In summary, market and investment barriers to circular and NBS stem from structural misalignments, valuation challenges, and institutional unfamiliarity. Addressing these barriers will require improved data and metrics, supportive policy frameworks, financial innovation, and targeted efforts to build investor capacity and confidence in NBS as viable, scalable, and resilient investment opportunities.

Blended Finance, Green Bonds, and Valuation Tools

Scaling the implementation of NBS and circular design approaches requires innovative financial instruments and tools that can address market failures, reduce investment risk, and accurately capture the full value of ecosystem services. Among the most promising mechanisms are blended finance structures, green bonds, and ecosystem service valuation tools. These instruments support the mobilization of public and private capital, improve project bankability, and integrate environmental value into investment decision-making frameworks.

Blended Finance

Blended finance refers to the strategic use of public or philanthropic funding to attract private sector investment into projects that deliver environmental and social benefits. It addresses key market barriers such as perceived risk, limited returns, and high upfront costs by combining concessional capital with commercial finance. In the context of NBS and circular initiatives, blended finance can make projects more investable by absorbing first losses, guaranteeing returns, or covering development and transaction costs.

Public institutions—including development banks, climate funds, and national governments—can use blended finance to de-risk NBS by providing subordinated loans, guarantees, or grants that increase investor confidence. For example, a development bank might provide concessional funding for watershed restoration, while private investors finance water infrastructure that benefits from improved hydrological stability. This layered approach reduces exposure for private investors while enabling larger volumes of capital to flow into complex or untested project models.

Blended finance can also help aggregate smaller-scale NBS initiatives—such as community greening, urban gardens, or decentralized water systems—into larger portfolios. Aggregation mechanisms, such as project bundling or special purpose vehicles, allow smaller investments to meet the scale thresholds required by institutional investors, thereby increasing access to capital and lowering transaction costs.

Green Bonds

Green bonds are debt instruments used to raise funds for projects that deliver environmental benefits. As the green finance market expands, green bonds have become a widely accepted tool for financing climate-aligned infrastructure, including renewable energy, energy efficiency, and, increasingly, NBS. The proceeds from green bonds are earmarked for specific uses, and issuers are required to report on the environmental outcomes of the financed activities.

Issuers of green bonds include governments, municipalities, development banks, and corporations. When used to fund NBS, green bonds can support a variety of projects such as afforestation, wetland restoration, green urban infrastructure, and climate-resilient agriculture. For example, a city may issue a green bond to fund green roofs, permeable pavements, and bioswales as part of its stormwater management system. By framing these investments as environmentally beneficial, municipalities can access lower-cost capital, broaden their investor base, and signal climate commitment.

To ensure credibility, green bonds are typically aligned with international standards such as the Green Bond Principles or the Climate Bonds Standard. Independent verification and transparent reporting are essential for maintaining investor trust and market integrity. For NBS projects, this requires robust methodologies for estimating carbon sequestration, biodiversity outcomes, or avoided costs, which can be more complex than for traditional infrastructure.

The emerging field of sustainability-linked bonds, which tie repayment terms to performance on predefined sustainability metrics, presents additional opportunities for funding NBS. These bonds incentivize issuers to achieve environmental goals—such as increasing urban green cover or reducing water use—by offering interest rate reductions or other benefits upon meeting performance targets.

Valuation Tools

Accurate valuation of ecosystem services is fundamental to integrating NBS into financial planning and investment decisions. Traditional cost-benefit analysis often underestimates the value of natural systems because it does not capture non-market benefits or account for long-term ecological and social outcomes. Valuation tools help quantify and communicate the full economic, social, and environmental value of NBS, supporting more informed decision-making by public and private actors.

Several approaches have been developed to value ecosystem services. These include:

- Revealed preference methods, which infer value based on actual behavior, such as the price people are willing to pay for housing near green spaces.
- Stated preference methods, such as contingent valuation and choice experiments, which ask individuals directly how much they value certain ecosystem services.
- Avoided cost methods, which estimate the value of services based on the costs that would be incurred if they were lost—for example, the cost of building flood barriers to replace wetland functions.
- Replacement cost methods, which assess how much it would cost to replace ecosystem services with engineered alternatives.

These tools are increasingly supported by spatial analysis platforms and environmental-economic accounting frameworks, such as the System of Environmental-Economic Accounting—Ecosystem Accounting (SEEA-EA). These frameworks enable the integration of natural capital values into national accounts, development plans, and corporate reporting.

Natural capital valuation can also be embedded into project appraisal tools used by investors, development banks, and infrastructure planners. For example, NBS can be assessed based on lifecycle cost analysis that includes environmental externalities, resilience co-benefits, and avoided damages. Incorporating these factors helps demonstrate the comparative advantage of NBS over grey infrastructure, particularly when long-term benefits are considered.

In addition, digital tools such as GIS-based models, ecosystem service mapping, and remote sensing enhance the accuracy and usability of valuation data. These technologies allow for more precise estimation of NBS performance, visualization of trade-offs, and integration into planning processes.

Enabling Conditions

To unlock the full potential of blended finance, green bonds, and valuation tools for NBS, certain enabling conditions are required. These include:

- **Policy and regulatory support**: Clear definitions, eligibility criteria, and performance standards for NBS within climate, biodiversity, and finance frameworks.
- **Institutional capacity**: Technical expertise within public agencies, financial institutions, and project developers to design, implement, and evaluate NBS investments.
- **Data infrastructure**: Accessible, reliable data on ecosystem conditions, service flows, and project performance to support valuation and reporting.
- **Partnerships**: Collaboration among public, private, and civil society actors to co-develop financing structures and leverage diverse resources.

Conclusion

Blended finance, green bonds, and valuation tools provide critical mechanisms for bridging financing gaps and advancing investment in circular and nature-based systems. By addressing risk, improving return profiles, and articulating the value of ecosystem services, these instruments create pathways for aligning financial flows with sustainability and resilience objectives. Their broader adoption, supported by enabling frameworks and institutional capacity, will be essential for mainstreaming NBS in infrastructure planning and development finance.

Sustainable Finance as a Driver of Circularity

Sustainable finance plays a critical role in enabling the transition from linear models of development to circular systems that prioritize resource efficiency, ecological regeneration, and long-term resilience. By aligning financial flows with environmental, social, and governance (ESG) objectives, sustainable finance provides both the capital and the strategic orientation needed to scale circular economy practices, including NBS. As financial institutions increasingly recognize the material risks posed by environmental degradation and climate change, sustainable finance is emerging as a key driver of systemic change.

At its core, sustainable finance refers to investment and lending decisions that incorporate ESG considerations into risk assessment, portfolio construction, and capital allocation. This includes financing projects that contribute to climate mitigation and adaptation, biodiversity conservation, pollution reduction, and sustainable resource use. The circular economy, with its focus on reducing waste, extending product life cycles, and closing material loops, aligns well with the objectives of sustainable finance.

One way sustainable finance supports circularity is through the development of financial products and instruments that explicitly target circular outcomes. Green loans, sustainability-linked loans, and impact investment funds are being tailored to support businesses and public entities pursuing circular models. These instruments can be used to finance activities such as remanufacturing, recycling infrastructure, sustainable product design, and regenerative agriculture. In many cases, financing terms are linked to the achievement of measurable sustainability outcomes, incentivizing performance and accountability.

Sustainable finance also promotes circularity through the integration of ESG metrics into investment analysis and corporate disclosure. Investors are increasingly using circularity indicators—such as material efficiency, waste reduction, and resource recovery—as part of their due diligence processes. Companies and municipalities that adopt circular practices and can demonstrate measurable benefits are more likely to attract investment and secure favorable financing conditions. As ESG reporting standards evolve, the inclusion of circular economy performance data is likely to become more common.

Institutional investors, including pension funds and sovereign wealth funds, are beginning to view circular investments as a strategy for reducing long-term exposure to resource volatility, regulatory risk, and reputational concerns. Financing projects that reduce reliance on virgin materials, improve supply chain resilience, or regenerate degraded ecosystems is consistent with fiduciary responsibilities focused on long-term value preservation.

Policy and regulatory frameworks also reinforce the connection between sustainable finance and circularity. Taxonomies developed by governments and international bodies—such as the EU Sustainable Finance Taxonomy—identify circular economy activities as eligible for sustainable investment. These frameworks provide clarity to investors, reduce greenwashing risks, and help guide capital toward projects with genuine environmental benefits.

In summary, sustainable finance serves as both an enabler and accelerator of circular economy transitions. By providing targeted capital, shaping market incentives, and embedding ESG considerations into financial decision-making, sustainable finance creates the conditions for circular and nature-based approaches to flourish. Continued development of standards, tools, and partnerships will be essential to further integrate circularity into the mainstream of sustainable investment practices.

Chapter 9: Designing Circular NBS for Community and Equity

This chapter explores how circular NBS can be designed to promote inclusion, social equity, and community empowerment. While NBS and circular systems offer environmental and economic benefits, their success also depends on how fairly these benefits are distributed and how meaningfully communities are engaged in the design and management of such interventions.

Socioeconomic vulnerabilities, spatial inequalities, and institutional barriers can limit access to NBS, reinforcing existing disparities. Inclusive design and co-creation approaches aim to address these challenges by prioritizing community leadership, recognizing diverse needs, and embedding equity into planning and implementation processes.

The chapter outlines strategies for closing equity gaps, fostering local stewardship, and supporting community-driven innovation. It emphasizes that empowering communities through regenerative systems is essential not only for justice and inclusion but also for the long-term effectiveness and resilience of circular NBS.

Equity Gaps in Access to NBS

Equity gaps in access to NBS are a growing concern as cities and regions adopt these approaches to address climate and environmental challenges. While NBS offer wide-ranging benefits—including improved air and water quality, flood protection, temperature regulation, and enhanced well-being—these benefits are not distributed evenly across populations or geographies. Structural inequalities related to income, race, ethnicity, gender, disability, and geographic location often determine who benefits from NBS and who remains underserved or excluded.

One key aspect of equity gaps is spatial inequality. In many urban areas, green spaces and other forms of NBS are concentrated in wealthier neighborhoods, while lower-income or historically marginalized communities may experience limited access to parks, street trees, or green infrastructure. This disparity affects residents' exposure to environmental hazards such as extreme heat or flooding and limits their ability to benefit from the physical and mental health advantages associated with proximity to nature.

Historical patterns of exclusion and disinvestment have contributed to these spatial gaps. In some cases, planning decisions, zoning policies, or infrastructure investments have disproportionately favored certain areas while neglecting others. For example, the placement of industrial facilities or transportation corridors has often occurred near low-income neighborhoods, increasing environmental burdens while limiting access to restorative green spaces. These legacies continue to shape patterns of access to NBS today.

Socioeconomic barriers also play a role in limiting access. Even when nature-based amenities are located nearby, individuals may face constraints such as lack of time, transportation, safety concerns, or limited cultural relevance of public spaces. These barriers reduce the extent to which certain populations can use and benefit from NBS. Additionally, language, information access, and exclusion from decision-making processes can reinforce marginalization, leaving some communities out of NBS planning and design efforts altogether.

Equity gaps can also emerge in rural and peri-urban areas, where residents may live close to natural landscapes but lack the infrastructure, investment, or institutional support needed to benefit from NBS. For example, smallholder farmers or Indigenous communities may rely on ecosystem services for their livelihoods yet face challenges in securing land tenure, technical assistance, or financing for restoration and conservation efforts.

Furthermore, climate adaptation and resilience strategies that involve NBS may unintentionally exacerbate inequities if they trigger land value increases, green gentrification, or displacement of vulnerable populations. Without safeguards, well-intentioned projects can contribute to exclusion by increasing housing costs or altering neighborhood dynamics in ways that disadvantage long-standing residents.

Addressing equity gaps in NBS access requires deliberate, inclusive planning and governance practices. This includes prioritizing investment in underserved areas, incorporating community voices in project design, and tailoring interventions to reflect diverse cultural, social, and ecological contexts. Metrics and monitoring tools that track distributional outcomes can support more equitable implementation and help ensure that NBS contribute to both environmental and social sustainability.

In summary, equity gaps in access to NBS are shaped by intersecting social, economic, and spatial factors. Ensuring fair and inclusive access to the benefits of NBS is essential for advancing climate justice and building resilient, healthy communities.

Socioeconomic Vulnerability and Exclusion

Socioeconomic vulnerability plays a significant role in shaping who benefits from environmental interventions, including NBS and circular infrastructure. Vulnerability is not solely a function of exposure to environmental risks, but also reflects underlying social and economic conditions that influence individuals' and communities' capacity to prepare for, respond to, and recover from environmental stressors. When these vulnerabilities are not adequately addressed in the design and implementation of NBS, they can reinforce patterns of exclusion and inequality.

Communities facing socioeconomic vulnerability often contend with multiple, overlapping disadvantages—such as low income, limited access to education, insecure employment, housing instability, and

94

limited political representation. These factors can restrict access to decision-making processes, reduce awareness of environmental programs, and limit the ability to benefit from or contribute to sustainability initiatives. For example, households facing financial constraints may be unable to participate in community-based NBS projects that require time, tools, or space, even if such projects are designed to be inclusive.

Exclusion can also occur through institutional processes that inadvertently prioritize technical or financial efficiency over equity. Planning and development mechanisms may focus on areas with the highest return on investment, easiest implementation pathways, or lowest perceived risk, leaving out communities that require more engagement, support, or tailored approaches. In doing so, well-intentioned NBS interventions may neglect or bypass vulnerable populations, further marginalizing those already at risk.

Furthermore, limited tenure security and lack of formal recognition of informal settlements or customary land rights can prevent communities from accessing the benefits of NBS or participating in circular development strategies. In urban contexts, residents of informal settlements may be excluded from municipal greening initiatives or face displacement pressures when land values rise following NBS investments. In rural areas, smallholder farmers or Indigenous communities may struggle to access support for regenerative practices if land tenure is contested or undocumented.

Language, cultural norms, and information asymmetry also shape patterns of inclusion and exclusion. Public consultations, outreach campaigns, and project materials are often not translated into multiple languages or adapted to local contexts, which can limit participation among non-dominant or minority groups. When communication barriers persist, vulnerable communities may be unaware of the opportunities that NBS can offer or may mistrust external actors proposing environmental interventions.

Another layer of exclusion relates to gender and caregiving roles. Women and caregivers often bear disproportionate responsibility for household and community well-being, especially in lower-income settings. However, their voices may be underrepresented in formal planning processes or decision-making bodies. If NBS are designed without considering gender-specific needs, such as accessibility, safety, and social infrastructure, they may fail to meet the priorities of these groups or reinforce unequal burdens.

Importantly, exclusion is not always intentional but can result from a lack of inclusive design, participation, and evaluation frameworks. Without mechanisms to assess who benefits from NBS and who is left out, projects may unintentionally reproduce or intensify existing disparities. This is particularly critical in areas facing climate-related risks, where adaptation measures must serve all residents equitably to be effective.

Addressing socioeconomic vulnerability and exclusion in NBS planning requires a proactive, equity-centered approach. This includes identifying at-risk groups early in the planning process, allocating resources to enable meaningful participation, and designing flexible interventions that respond to local needs and capacities. It also involves monitoring impacts over time to ensure that benefits are distributed fairly and that emerging inequalities are identified and addressed.

In summary, socioeconomic vulnerability shapes access to and outcomes from NBS. Without deliberate action to address exclusion, sustainability interventions may fall short of their goals or worsen disparities. Embedding equity into NBS design and implementation is therefore essential for achieving inclusive and resilient environmental solutions.

Inclusive Circular Design and Co-Creation Approaches

Inclusive circular design and co-creation approaches are central to ensuring that circular economy initiatives and NBS are equitable, socially responsive, and reflective of the needs and priorities of diverse communities. These approaches emphasize the involvement of stakeholders—particularly those who are typically underrepresented—in all stages of project development, from concept and planning to implementation, governance, and monitoring. When integrated effectively, inclusive design and co-creation contribute to more resilient outcomes, foster local ownership, and reduce the risk of exclusion or unintended negative consequences.

Circular design, in its technical sense, refers to systems that maintain the value of materials and resources by minimizing waste and maximizing reuse, recycling, and regeneration. However, when applied without consideration of social dynamics, circular interventions can overlook who benefits from resource flows, who bears the burdens, and who is left out. Inclusive circular design aims to address these gaps by embedding equity, participation, and justice into the design of circular systems.

A foundational principle of inclusive circular design is accessibility—ensuring that the physical, economic, and social benefits of circular systems are available to all. This includes equitable access to green infrastructure, public services such as composting or waste collection, and opportunities for economic participation in circular value chains. For example, repair and reuse centers, urban farming cooperatives, and resource recovery initiatives can be designed to provide employment opportunities and affordable services for underserved communities.

Co-creation, in this context, refers to collaborative processes through which stakeholders jointly identify problems, develop solutions, and make decisions. It recognizes that people have unique knowledge about their environments, needs, and priorities that is critical for effective and context-appropriate design. Co-creation is not limited to consultation; it involves shared authority and responsibility across diverse actors, including community members, local authorities, technical experts, non-profit organizations, and private sector partners.

Effective co-creation processes begin with early engagement. Rather than bringing communities into projects after key decisions have been made, inclusive circular design involves stakeholders from the outset, shaping the goals, design principles, and criteria for success. This helps build trust, increases legitimacy, and reduces the likelihood of conflict or resistance during implementation. It also ensures that the resulting systems align with local values, cultural norms, and day-to-day realities.

To enable meaningful participation, co-creation must address barriers to engagement, such as language, time constraints, access to information, or previous experiences of marginalization. This requires inclusive facilitation methods—such as multilingual workshops, culturally appropriate materials, flexible meeting times, and child-friendly venues. It also involves recognizing and valuing different forms of knowledge, including traditional ecological knowledge, lived experience, and informal expertise.

Design justice frameworks can guide inclusive circular design by focusing attention on who is included in design processes, whose voices are prioritized, and how benefits and risks are distributed. This perspective encourages designers and planners to reflect on their own positions, challenge dominant assumptions, and support decision-making that redistributes power. For example, applying design justice principles might lead a city to prioritize NBS investments in historically underserved neighborhoods or to engage informal waste workers in developing resource recovery systems.

Another important consideration is intersectionality—the recognition that people's identities and experiences are shaped by multiple, overlapping factors such as gender, age, race, disability, and income. Intersectional approaches to circular design acknowledge that vulnerability and exclusion are not uniform and that inclusive solutions must accommodate diverse needs and capacities. For example, green public spaces may need to incorporate safety features, seating, and inclusive programming to ensure that they are welcoming and usable by elderly residents, women, children, and people with disabilities.

Governance arrangements also play a role in supporting co-creation and inclusivity. Participatory governance structures—such as advisory committees, community oversight groups, and stakeholder networks—create formal mechanisms for shared decision-making and accountability. When these structures have clear mandates, transparent processes, and equitable representation, they can support sustained collaboration and ensure that circular systems remain responsive to community needs over time.

Capacity-building is essential for enabling co-creation, particularly in communities that have been historically marginalized or have limited resources. This includes supporting technical skills development, providing access to planning tools and data, and creating opportunities for leadership and advocacy. Capacity-building efforts should be reciprocal, with institutions also learning from communities and adapting their practices accordingly.

Monitoring and evaluation frameworks should include equity and inclusion indicators to assess how well circular and NBS interventions are meeting their social goals. This may involve tracking distributional outcomes (e.g. who benefits from new infrastructure), procedural outcomes (e.g. who participates in governance), and recognition outcomes (e.g. whose knowledge and values are reflected in decision-making). These metrics help identify gaps, guide course corrections, and build accountability.

Examples of inclusive circular design and co-creation are increasingly found in practice. Initiatives such as community-designed green spaces, neighborhood composting schemes, and participatory budgeting for sustainability projects illustrate the potential of these approaches. While outcomes vary, they consistently show that inclusion leads to more innovative, durable, and widely supported interventions.

Challenges remain, including time constraints, power imbalances, and institutional inertia. Co-creation can be resource-intensive and requires a shift in organizational culture and expectations. However, the long-term benefits—more equitable outcomes, greater resilience, and stronger community engagement—demonstrate its value as a core element of sustainable systems transformation.

In conclusion, inclusive circular design and co-creation approaches are essential for ensuring that circular economy and NBS initiatives contribute to environmental and social justice. By embedding equity, participation, and responsiveness into the design process, these approaches help create systems that are not only efficient and regenerative but also inclusive and empowering for all stakeholders.

Empowering Communities Through Regenerative Systems

Regenerative systems aim to restore and enhance the capacity of social and ecological systems to thrive over time. When applied through a community-centered lens, these systems offer opportunities to empower individuals and groups by increasing local agency, resilience, and participation in sustainable development processes. Empowering communities through regenerative systems involves more than delivering environmental outcomes—it includes building skills, strengthening networks, and supporting the conditions for long-term self-determination.

At the core of this empowerment is community ownership of resources and decision-making. Regenerative systems are most effective when designed and managed by those who directly depend on and interact with the environment. This local stewardship enhances place-based knowledge and fosters a sense of responsibility for long-term outcomes. Whether managing a community forest, maintaining urban green infrastructure, or coordinating a circular food system, community-led models ensure that interventions are grounded in local priorities and adaptive to changing conditions.

Capacity-building is essential for enabling communities to participate meaningfully in regenerative efforts. This includes developing technical knowledge about circular practices, ecological restoration, and climate adaptation, as well as strengthening organizational and leadership skills. Workshops, peer-learning networks, and partnerships with academic or non-governmental institutions can support community members in designing, implementing, and monitoring regenerative projects. These skills are transferable, expanding opportunities for employment and entrepreneurship in emerging green and circular sectors.

Economic empowerment is another important dimension. Regenerative systems can support local livelihoods by creating jobs in ecological restoration, waste recovery, sustainable agriculture, and green infrastructure maintenance. Community enterprises—such as composting cooperatives, repair hubs, or resource-sharing platforms—offer pathways for inclusive economic participation, especially when barriers to entry are minimized and revenue is reinvested locally. These models contribute to economic resilience by diversifying income sources and reducing reliance on external markets.

In addition to tangible benefits, regenerative systems foster social cohesion and well-being. Shared responsibility for managing green spaces, circular resource systems, or community energy projects can strengthen relationships, increase trust, and promote collective action. These social benefits are particularly valuable in communities facing environmental or economic stress, where inclusive, collaborative efforts can serve as a foundation for broader resilience.

Policy and institutional support play a vital role in enabling community empowerment through regenerative systems. Legal frameworks that recognize community rights to manage natural resources, funding mechanisms that support grassroots innovation, and planning processes that incorporate local input are all essential. These supports help shift power toward communities and ensure that regenerative approaches are not imposed but co-created and sustained over time.

In summary, empowering communities through regenerative systems involves creating opportunities for meaningful participation, capacity development, and equitable access to benefits. When communities are supported to lead in designing and managing regenerative initiatives, the resulting systems are more likely to be inclusive, adaptive, and enduring. This empowerment is not only an outcome of regenerative practice—it is a prerequisite for its success.

Conclusion

NBS and circular design represent two complementary approaches that offer practical pathways toward regenerative, resilient, and sustainable systems. As this book has outlined, the integration of these frameworks can address complex environmental challenges—including climate change, biodiversity loss, and resource depletion—while simultaneously delivering social and economic benefits. When implemented with care, inclusivity, and long-term vision, circular NBS can support systems that are not only environmentally sound but also equitable and adaptive.

The shift from linear to circular thinking requires reimagining how societies produce, consume, and manage natural resources. Circular systems seek to minimize waste and regenerate value through closed loops, while NBS work with natural processes to restore and enhance ecosystem functions. Together, they provide a foundation for transforming infrastructure, land use, governance, and finance in ways that align with ecological limits and support multifunctional outcomes.

A recurring theme throughout this book is the need for systemic change—moving beyond fragmented responses to integrated, cross-sectoral strategies. Governance models that enable collaboration across institutions, disciplines, and spatial scales are necessary to coordinate policies, align investments, and ensure that solutions are context-specific and responsive. Institutionalizing circular NBS involves embedding their principles into planning processes, regulatory frameworks, financing structures, and everyday decision-making.

Financing remains a significant barrier, but it also presents an opportunity for innovation. Blended finance, green bonds, and natural capital valuation tools are helping to bridge funding gaps and demonstrate the long-term value of circular and nature-based approaches. As sustainable finance frameworks continue to evolve, there is increasing potential to align capital flows with regenerative development goals.

Inclusion and equity are critical to the success of circular NBS. Without deliberate efforts to address socioeconomic vulnerabilities and historic patterns of exclusion, these solutions may fall short or even exacerbate disparities. Inclusive design, co-creation, and community empowerment are essential strategies for ensuring that NBS reflect diverse perspectives and that benefits are shared equitably. Regenerative systems that are designed and managed with communities—not just for them—are more likely to endure and adapt over time.

Looking ahead, the challenge is not only to scale individual projects but to mainstream regenerative thinking across institutions, sectors, and regions. This includes fostering a culture of collaboration, supporting capacity-building, and developing policy frameworks that reward long-term value over short-term returns. Research, innovation, and monitoring will also play important roles in refining methodologies, tracking progress, and communicating outcomes to a wide range of stakeholders.

In conclusion, the convergence of nature-based and circular approaches offers a compelling vision for the future—one that recognizes the interdependence of human and natural systems and seeks to create conditions in which both can thrive. By embracing this integration, decision-makers, practitioners, and communities can contribute to a more sustainable, just, and regenerative world.

www.ingramcontent.com/pod-product-compliance
Lightning Source LLC
Chambersburg PA
CBHW052140270326
41930CB00012B/2960